THE GREAT OUTCRY
for the
TRUE GOSPEL
THIS ERA

THE GREAT OUTCRY
for the
TRUE GOSPEL
THIS ERA

Jango Emmanuel Fortty

authorHOUSE®

AuthorHouse™
1663 Liberty Drive
Bloomington, IN 47403
www.authorhouse.com
Phone: 1 (800) 839-8640

Published by AuthorHouse 08/20/2015

ISBN: 978-1-5049-2726-0 (sc)
ISBN: 978-1-5049-2724-6 (e)

Library of Congress Control Number: 2015912582

Scripture quotations marked KJV are from the Holy Bible, King James Version (Authorized Version). First published in 1611. Quoted from the KJV Classic Reference Bible, Copyright © 1983 by The Zondervan Corporation.

Print information available on the last page.

Any people depicted in stock imagery provided by Thinkstock are models, and such images are being used for illustrative purposes only. Certain stock imagery © Thinkstock.

This book is printed on acid-free paper.

CONTENTS

OH HOW ARE WE HAVE FALLEN (WE THAT ARE MEMBERS OF THE BODY OF CHRIST)

On Friday morning, in May 2014, I was seated in the Kapucijnenvoer Garden of Leuven, Belgium. That is where I did most of my thinking. I would go there regularly during the day and just sit alone, planning my future steps. Today was a day of its kind. The weather was reasonable, a little breezy, but good enough for the thinking business. I had migrated from Milan Italy when God expressively told me that He would provide documents for me, the Italian Permesso di Soggiorno. This would make my stay in Europe legal, and thereafter, God will help me prosper. Indeed, I was granted a three-year subsidiary protection in July 2012 in Milan. Due to the crisis Italy was facing during this period, I decided to move to Belgium after seeking God's counsel.

I was seated alone, thoughts racing through my mind. God promised to prosper me after giving me a resident permit in Europe, but three years would soon be over, and I would have to go back to Italy to renew this document. After scanning the whole of Belgium, I still could find no job. My Italian subsidiary protection document was rejected every time, because companies preferred to employ people with Belgian documents or with a passport from a European Union's country. Employing me would cost them a huge amount of government tax, and the process was complex and tiring. Again, I was trapped in a crude system that tied people's destinies to a piece of paper. No, not me,

I said to myself, life is a spiritual battle, in which man desperately seeks to enslave and use man, but we have a choice to say No when we ought to and YES when we ought to, that the message will be transferred to our Spirit man who fights our spiritual battles for us then we become victorious and it becomes manifested in the earthly realm. And NO I said. No system will hold me down, no system whatsoever because I have the Lord God Almighty within me. He is the invisible conqueror of every tough and rugged situation I found myself in.

Time has proven this, but what was I to do, what was the way out and forward? I was troubled, mainly with pressure from back home from my relatives and friends who needed financial assistance. God had not yet opened a financial door for me and I was living only on hand to mouth. The promises of God never fail, but waiting can be highly difficult in a world faced with challenges and demands to meet. "Thou should not bother this much," was the response I heard soon after. A gentle and comforting inner voice reminding me of Habakkuk 2:1-4

1 I will stand upon my watch, and set me upon the tower, and will watch th see what He will say unto me, and what I shall answer when I am reproved.

2 And the Lord answered me, and said, write the vision and make it plain upon tables, that he may run that readeth it.

3 For the vision is yet for an appointed time, but at the end it shall speak, and not lie: though it tarry, wait for it, because it will not tarry.

4 Behold, his soul which is lifted up is not upright in him: but the just shall live by faith.

God's promises are always fulfilled in His perfect timing, but it has never been a bread and butter business. I chatted alone with my thoughts, considering men like Joseph and David in the Bible who suffered greatly before God's promises were fulfilled, leading them to walk into the peace of their visions. My thoughts were interrupted by a tall, huge black man in his late forties. With a majestic approach and his eyes fixed on my dreamy eyes, he greeted me, "Hello bro." I have a message for you he said, so I welcomed him to take a seat. He noted that as he was passing by, he felt guided and inspired to approach me and tell me that God will prosper me greatly, but that I should trust in Him. He encouraged me to attend his church by faith and watch God's promise in my life come true. He said other things too, but these two points obtained my attention the most:

1) That God intends to prosper me greatly.
2) That I should act in faith and start coming to his church.

I have heard the promises of God over and over, directly from Him and indirectly from men of God. The only thing that bothered me is that he said in order for the promises to come true in my life, I must act in faith by going to his church. Oh my, I thought, could this be another church member seeking men like most others out there? Once again, I got myself worked up as thoughts raced through my mind; even more so, for the fact that in the past six months, I had visited up to ten churches, including the one he was inviting me to. I always left with a heavy heart, for the preaching always advanced towards the direction of money and bringing people back to the fulfilled things of the Old which we have been liberated. The Souls of the innocent flock grew more hungry and thirsty for the true message of salvation, the message of Christ and His cross, yet no none or just a few true shepherd noticed that. Whereas this, and this alone, is what we truly need for our salvation in this era which is of grace in Jesus Christ. This was a heavy burden to bear as my Spirit was troubled every time I came across money seeking wolves of preachers and a body of people that were needy. I would ask myself countless questions. God, why do you allow such things to happen? Why are you silent when dishonesty takes place in your house? Aren't you the same God today that was yesterday? The Bible says in Mathew 7:15-23

15 Beware of false prophets, which come to you in sheep's clothing, but inwardly they are ravening wolves.

16 Ye shall know them by their fruits. Do men gather grapes of thorns, or figs of thistles?

17 Even so every good tree bringeth forth good fruit; but a corrupt tree bringeth forth evil fruit.

18 A good tree cannot forth evil fruit, neither can a corrupt tree bring forth good fruit.

19 Every tree that bringeth not forth good fruit is hewn down, and cast into the fire.

20 Wherefore by their fruits ye shall know them.

21 Not every one that saith unto me, Lord, Lord, shall enter into heaven; but he that doeth the will of my Father which is in heaven.

22 Many will say to me in that day, Lord, Lord have we not prophesied in thy name? And in thy name have cast out devils? And in thy name done many wonderful works?

23 And then will I profess unto them, I never knew you: depart from me, ye that work iniquity.

I took special note of verses 16 and 17. Christ was in essence saying that we appreciate a preacher based solely on the fruit that comes out of him. The fruit Christ was talking about reflects the words that come out of them in the form of preaching. The question worth posing here is, "What are good fruits versus bad fruits?" Bad fruits in this context will consist of preaching that demands us to do this or that in order to guarantee our salvation and compensate Christ for our redemption. This is misleading and the opposite of good fruit-like preaching, which talks about the fact that we all acquire in this era of the New Testament, which is solely built upon GRACE. It can simply be defined as unmerited favor granted to us by Christ upon His precious Cross. This and this alone is our sole requirement. The great Apostle Paul says in 1 Corinthians 1:

1 Corinthians 1: 17-24

17 For Christ sent me not to baptize, but to preach the gospel: not with wisdom of words, lest the cross of Christ should be made of none effect.

18 For the preaching of the cross is to them that perish foolishness; but unto us which are saved it is the power of God.

19 For it is written, I will destroy the wisdom of the wise, and will bring to nothing the understanding of the prudent.

20 Where is the wise? Where is the scribe? Where is the disputer of this world? hath not God made foolish the wisdom of this world?

21 For after that in the wisdom of God the world by wisdom knew not God, it pleased God by the foolishness of preaching to save them that believe.

22 For the Jews require a sign, and the Greeks seek after wisdom:

23 But we preach Christ crucified, unto the Jews a stumbling block, and unto the Greeks foolishness.

24 But unto them which are called, both Jews and Greeks, Christ the power of God, and the wisdom of God.

Sometimes when I read such passages of the Bible, I wonder whether it makes no sense to us, we don't get the message because we have allowed ourselves to be blinded by our own misleading lusts. This is what we need brethren, the wisdom of Christ. 2 Timothy 3:15 says;

15 And that from a child thou hast known the holy scriptures, which are able to make thee wise unto salvation through faith which is in Christ Jesus

King Solomon, even in the shadow era, was wise enough to sweep the Almighty off His feet to prompt action of giving him wisdom beyond comprehension. That caused men, kings and queens from far and wide to bring good tidings to him so that they may hear him speak. We, brethren, are beloved children of God, privileged to operate in this gracious era as Christians. What do we do with this grace? Do we pray for wisdom to discern what really is or do we set it aside and make irrelevance out of it? The wisdom of Christ is God's all in all and it relates to true freedom and salvation. Great Apostle Paul said in Romans 1:16;

16 For I am not ashamed of the gospel of Christ: for it is the power of God unto salvation to everyone that believeth; to the Jews first, and then to the Greek.

This and this alone is all we need. Rejecting this and expecting something better is directly saying that the wisdom of God is foolish. Brethren, it is a complex thing and takes grace to grasp it. No wonder

Christ responded in this manner when His apostles questioned why He spoke to the crowd in parables in Mathew 13:10-17;

10 And the disciples came, and said unto him, why speakest thou unto them in parables?

11 He answered and said unto them, Because it is given unto you to know the mysteries of the kingdom of heaven, but them it is not given.

12 For whosoever hath, to him shall be given, and he shall have more abundance: but whosoever hath not, from him shall be taken away, even that he hath.

13 Therefore speak I to them in parables: because seeing they see not, and hearing they hear not, neither do they understand.

14 And in them is fulfilled the prophecy of Esaias, which saith: By hearing ye shall hear, and shall not understand; and seeing ye shall see, and shall not perceive:

15 For this people's heart is waxed gross, and their ears are dull of hearing, and their eyes they have closed; lest at any time they should see with their eyes and hear with their ears, and should understand with their hearts, and should be converted, and I should heal them.

16 But blessed are your eyes, for they see: and your ears, for they hear.

17 For verily I say unto you that many prophets and righteous men have desired to see those things which ye see, and have not seen them; and to hear those things which ye hear, and have not heard them.

The wisdom of God is a hidden mystery revealed to some and withheld from others. By the grace of God, the humble are given more than the proud. Receiving and comprehending a hidden mystery is a gift in itself, but some have pitifully fallen from this blessed grace due to their own cravings. Great apostle Paul in his second letter to Timothy says;

2 Timothy 4:3-5

3 For the time will come when they will not endure sound doctrine; but after their own lusts shall they heap to themselves teachers, having itching ears;

4 And they shall turn away their ears from the truth, and shall be turned unto fables.

5 But watch thou in all things, endure afflictions, do the work of an evangelist, make full proof of thy ministry.

Today, if men are to please God, they must reject all human traditions. They should not only say no to the lusts of their own flesh, but they should actually learn how to say no and pray for the grace of God to see them through. Jesus said to the Scribes and Pharisees, "You make void the commandment of God by your tradition, which you have handed down; and many suchlike things you do." (Mark 7:13). Paul said, "Hence rebuke them sharply that they may be sound in the faith, and may not listen to Jewish fables and commandments of men who turn from the truth." (Titus 1:13-14). Again Paul said, "See to it that no one deceives you by philosophy and vain deceit, according to human traditions, according to the elements of the world and not according to Christ." (Colossians 2:8). Hence, the Bible repeatedly warns against adhering to traditions of men. In spite of this, the Church has an abundance of human traditions and continually seeks to justify them. When God says one thing, they say another.

It has been my immense desire to see a genuine revival with God's own Hand upon it. I am not talking about revival of financial breakthroughs or miracles that satisfy the greed of people, like the crowd to which Jesus was preaching in John 14, 15 and 16. Nor that which seeks to bring more members into the Church with a selfish hidden agenda of making money from the new converts. Rather, I want to see a revival that is orchestrated with the full zeal of Grace, to delve into the mind of God and download His true Word and desire for His people as salvation in this era of grace is concerned; to implant it into the minds and Spirits of His people who are still in bondage in their own ignorance and lack of wisdom.

Such men are easily identified; they are usually boastful and accord themselves with high titles. They project themselves as holy men, some put on white robes, others red and so on, with big crosses around their necks. Even in their speeches, they try to be soft and subtle, in their walking, they are the similitude of snails, some are even forbidden to marry, something highly honored by God; all in a bid to showcase themselves as most holy and righteous men in the eyes of the ignorant masses. Amidst all this, they are just the replica, the fruits and offspring of the Pharisees and scribes Jesus criticized exhaustively in the Book of Matthew 23.

Recently, I have come in contact with Anthony Todd, and David O'Conner of the United States of America, who are passionately pressing towards spreading the true word of God, and expose the viles of the devil through derailed and compromised. There are many more in America, Europe and Africa, but their voices are not heard because people's hearts have gone wild in search of the misleading voices that lie blatantly about God and collect huge chunks of euro and dollar bills from their victims. I am certain that someday true light will overcome darkness; that is the way it has always been. Until then, all that is yet to become history is still buried in tomorrow's time, cooking and bubbling up greatly like molten magma that will soon burst out wild.

For those who have watched the movie, 'The Ten Commandments,' there was a man working in the mud pit making bricks who was stabbed to death from a distance. All because he spoke up to an Egyptian soldier who was overseeing their work, ensuring that they labored ceaselessly. The victim questioned him, pointing out that they have deprived them of their bodies, must they also dishonor their women. When this happened, Moses rushed to the fallen man's side and held him in his arms, saying he will not allow a man to die in the mud. Before dying, the man told Moses that he had always prayed that God would show him the deliverer before he passes on.

He was in the hands of the deliverer but did not know it. God works through people and I will see the mighty hand of God in action, and will know that this is God himself at work and it will not be to me like a reality in some coded shadows like our brother in the mud pit. As these thoughts occupied my mind, an idea was dropped into my Spirit to write this book which by grace you are reading now. Through it, I can reach out to as many people as possible who thirst for truth. Yes, for the members of the Body of Christ have greatly fallen. There is an outcry from the Head (Christ) aimed at the Body (People), encouraging it to stand on its feet and return to its original position of knowing the Heavenly Father, in this glorious era through Christ. Oh, how we have fallen from such great height! Why? What is the cause? We have allowed ourselves to be taken away into the materialistic lusts of this world. This which Christ said is the root of all evil has drawn us completely from the love and wisdom of God.

I met an Italian guy, a friend who told me in the course of our First discussion that he was a PHD student in Theology. I was happy to hear that and I asked him why he preferred to study in Belgium instead of Italy. He said it was because of the money, that he could not find a job in Italy, so he chose to come over to Belgium. Here, they were paying him a good salary in the K U Leuven University, a salary of one thousand and eight hundred euros. He told me of a sheepish human success principle, which says go in first for the money, then think later, no wonder, he acted that way, his mind set as has always been the case was expressed in his words. Look people, there is no such thing as go in first then think about the things of God last. Better to embrace your calling and work for God out of love or stay completely out of the business. No wonder when I asked him what he intends to do after completing his PhD, his response was not to go into the streets and win lost Souls for God. No, his aim was to save as much money as he could, so he can go and develop his orange farm and earn a good life in Italy, and made no mention of the seed of love for God and for the lost. That is the motivator of ninety percent or more of today's preachers. That is why we hear them preach what they preach. Jeremiah 2:5 says;

5 Thus saith the Lord, what iniquity have your fathers found in me, that they are gone far from me, and have walked after vanity and are become vain?

Jeremiah was crying out to the children of God in Jerusalem who had turned away from God. It is important to note that idols does not only mean physical built structures, like baal, that people bow in front of to worship. It can refer to handed down beliefs and traditions from ages to ages that dwell in the hearts of men and have taken the place of God. It becomes a problem when people do not seek to glorify the Lord God Almighty and to magnify Christ as our only King and Savior. We should be aware of what we treasure in our hearts as this may have nothing to do with the will of God and His calling. The burning desire for lost Souls is either present or it has been compromised for the things of the world. This desire is like a seed God implants in His chosen people even before they are born. As they grow into the reality and understanding of the Word of God, so does the seed grow and awaken until it reaches its final stage of bringing forth good fruits. When this is absent in the Spirit of a man of God, it is obvious that he will be preaching out nothing but his own will. We know very well that as human beings, if not influenced by the Holy Spirit, we are naturally egoistic and greedy. There is no way we can fulfil the will of God if the will has not first been implanted within us. A vulture cannot give birth to a dove; neither can a wolf give birth to a sheep.

Several churches today, in Europe and America, seem to be headed by desperate money seekers and business men. With the Bible in their hands, they will do everything doable and undoable to steal the last penny out of an old homeless vagabond to add to the millions they have stolen already. Sad to think that some go to the extent of visiting witch doctors to get hypnotizing powers, electric rings and other equipment with which they can use to perform miracles to satisfy this money and miracle seeking generation. These people have sealed their Bibles, kept them forever new and buried within their boxes, and have refused to hold strong to God for revelation in His Word. We are no different today from the crowd Jesus was preaching to in the book of John 6. They insisted Jesus should give them physical bread like in the days of Moses when their forefathers ate manner from Heaven. They did not hear or perceive what Jesus was saying when He said that He was the true bread that came from the Father to replace the shadow bread Moses gave their forefathers. No, they did not embrace the mystery in this message, so decorated in glory, splendor and love, because the ears of their Spirit were sealed permanently with desire for tangible bread. Christ said in Matthew 12:39;

39 But he answered and said unto them, An evil and adulterous generation seeketh after a sign; and there shall no sign be given to it, but the sign of the prophet of Jonas.

The Bible says, ask and it shall be given unto you, seek and you shall find. I pray that God will help us seek like Solomon in this glorious era that we may find our way.

Notes and Reflections for Readers

Notes and Reflections for Readers

WHO ARE THE CHILDREN
OF GOD?

From the beginning of time, all who believed in God thought they were God's chosen people. Today, every denomination believes they are God's chosen people. This includes Catholics, Muslims, Jehovah Witnesses, all religions. The Jews believe that they have an ancient right to the claim of being God's chosen people. But do they? We need to view and understand who and what is a Jew. Are they Hebrews? Are they Israelites? Or are they just another religion? The first mention of the word Hebrew is in Genesis 14:13;

13 And there came one that had escaped, and told Abram the Hebrew; for he dwelt in the plain of Mamre the Amorite, brother of Eschol, and brother of Aner: and these were confederate with Abraham.

Abram or Abraham was a Hebrew. The word Hebrew comes from the word Heber or Eber and means, "The one from beyond or one who has passed over." The term Hebrew is a description of the patriarchs and the Israelites not of the Jews. The word Israelite comes from the word Israel. Jacob's name (the grandson of Abraham the Hebrew) was changed to Israel after he wrestled with the angel at Peniel. Jacob had ten sons before his name was changed to Israel. Two sons, Joseph and Benjamin, were born after his name was changed, but all the sons of Jacob were called the children of Israel. The word Israel means, "God prevails or he shall be a prince of God." A prince is the son of a king.

Those who are limited to carnal understanding would find it a mystery that God would refer to Israel as a prince. When they hear this, they expect some kind of physical prince to come out of Israel after Christ. No, God was not referring to physical princes, but spiritual ones that are born again through Christ. God handed the Ten Commandments and the laws to live by to the Israelites. There are two categories of creatures I would like us to examine as this will help us understand who the children of God are:

1) **The Creation of God**
2) **God's Chosen People**

THE CREATION OF GOD

Everything on earth, living and non-living, is God's creation. The air we breathe, water, and stones, etc. are all non-living things. Of the living things just to name a few, we have fish, birds, animals and human beings. Colossians 1:16 teaches us

16 For by him were all things created, that are in heaven, and that are in earth, visible and invisible, whether they be thrones, or dominions, or principalities, or powers: all things were created by him, and for him:

The Bible makes us understand that human beings are God's priority creation, top in ranking. We are created in God's image and are given the power to rule over all creation (Genesis 1:26). The Bible further makes us understand that God has given us dominion over all the powers, physical and spiritual of the earth; whether black or white, Jew or Gentile, we are all human beings in the sight of God and there is no ethnic discrimination in His sight. He has granted us free will and the power to subdue whether we are aware of it or not. There is a way to claim that authority which He has freely given to us. Colossians 2:10 tells us

10 And ye are complete in him, which is the head of all principality and power:

GOD'S CHOSEN PEOPLE

After the fall of man in Adam and Eve, God, after many centuries, introduced the law to the Israelites through Moses, a Levite of Israel. Man was supposed to keep this law in order to be free from the damnation that we are all born into as a result of the sin committed by our forefathers, Adam and Eve. We have close to 200 nations in the world, but God only picked one nation to gradually bring to light His predestined plan for man's salvation. Christ the Son, being Spirit, came on earth as a human being and went through the normal entrance of childbirth to accomplish His Godly purpose. God chose Mary and Joseph who were from the lineage of Abraham and had the promise of God.

Deuteronomy 7:6 says;

6 For thou art an holy people unto the Lord thy God: the Lord thy God hath chosen thee to be a special people unto Himself, above all people that are upon the face of the earth.

When man failed to keep the Ten Commandments that were introduced to him, through Moses, God sent forth His only begotten Son, Jesus Christ, as predestined, to do for us that which we could not do, so that through Him, we can be saved. Galatians 3:8-15 teaches us

8 And the scripture, forseeing that God would justify the heathen through faith, preached before the gospel unto Abraham, saying, in thee shall all nations be blessed.

9 So then they which be of faith are blessed with faithful Abraham.

10 For as many as are of the works of the law are under the curse; for it written, curse be anyone that continueth not in all things which are written in the book of the law, to do them.

11 But that no man is justified by the law in the sight of God, it is evident: for, The just shall live by faith.

12 And the law is not of faith: but, the man that doeth them shall live in them.

13 Christ hath redeemed us from the curse of the law, being made a curse for us: for it is written, cursed is every one that hangeth on a tree:

14 That the blessing of Abraham might come on the Gentiles through Christ; that we might receive the promise of the Spirit through faith.

15 Brethren, I speak after the manner of men; Though it be but a man's covenant, yet if it be confirmed, no man disannulleth, or addeth thereto.

We are told in the Book of 2 Samuel that David, a descendant of Abraham, born to the family of Jesse, was enthroned by God in place of Saul. David, a man after God's own heart, was so happy that God had given him rest from war from his surrounding neighbors. He thought about how unfair it was to live in a luxurious house built of cedar whilst the Ark of God was kept in a tent, so he told Nathan the Prophet that he desired to build a temple in which the Ark of God would be placed. Nathan encouraged him to do what was proposed in his heart, but that same night, the Word of God came to Nathan and said:

"Go and tell my servant David, 'This is what the LORD says: Are you the one to build me a house to dwell in? I have not dwelt in a house from the day I brought the Israelites up out of Egypt to this day. I have been moving from place to place with a tent as my dwelling. Wherever I have moved with all the Israelites, did I ever say to any of their rulers whom I commanded to shepherd my people Israel, "Why have you not built me a house of cedar?"'

"Now then, tell my servant David, 'This is what the LORD Almighty says: I took you from the pasture, from tending the flock, and appointed you ruler over my people Israel. I have been with you wherever you have gone, and I have cut off all your enemies from before you. Now I will make your name great, like the names of the greatest men on earth. And I will provide a place for my people Israel and will plant them so that they can have a home of their own and no longer be disturbed. Wicked people will not oppress them anymore, as they did at the beginning and have done ever since the time I appointed leaders over my people Israel. I will also give you rest from all your enemies.

"'The LORD declares to you that the LORD himself will establish a house for you: When your days are over and you rest with your ancestors, I will raise up your offspring to succeed you, your own flesh and blood, and I will establish his kingdom. He is the one who will build a house for my Name, and I will establish the throne of his kingdom forever. I will be his father, and he will be my son. When he does wrong, I will punish him with a rod wielded by men, with floggings inflicted by human hands. But my love will never be taken away from him, as I took it away from Saul, whom I removed from before you. Your house and your kingdom will endure forever before me; your throne will be established forever.'" (2 Samuel 7:5-16).

We see here that God, in response to the yearnings of David's heart, promised that out of the bowels of David shall come forth a king and God was to establish his kingdom forever. We may think that God was talking about Solomon who was the son of David and had a great kingdom, but no, the kingdom of Solomon passed away long ago. God, in one of His mystery speaking sessions, was referring to Our Lord and Savior, Jesus Christ who also came from the bowels of David, centuries after, and His kingdom has been, is still now and will be forever. All of us who are born again in Spirit are partakers of that glorious kingdom. Isaiah 9:6-7;

6 For unto us a child is born, unto us a son is given: and the government shall be upon his shoulder: and his name shall be called called Wonderful, councellor, The Mighty God, the everlasting Father, The prince of peace.

7 Of the increase of his government and peace there shall be no end, upon the throne of David, and upon his kingdom, to order it, and to establish it with judgement and with justice from henceforth even for ever. The zeal of the Lord of hosts will perform this.

In, Acts 13:22-23, we are told;

22 And when he had removed Him, he raised up unto them David to be their king; to whom also he gave their testimony, and said, I have found David the son of Jesse, a man after mine own heart, which shall fulfill all my will.

23 Of this man's seed hath God according to his promise raised unto Israel a savior, Jesus.

Our Lord who is Spirit came on earth as a man to fulfil that glorious promise which God made to Father Abraham in the Book of Genesis 12:1-3

1 Now the Lord had said unto Abram, Get thee out of thy country, and from thy kindred, and from thy father's house, unto a land that I will shew thee:

2 And I will make of thee a great nation, and I will bless thee, and make thy name great; and thou shalt be a blessing:

3 And I will bless them that thee, and curse him that curseth thee shall all families of the earth be blessed.

In the fourth chapter of Paul's letter to the Romans, we are told that Abraham, against all odds, believed in hope, that he will become the father of many nations according to that which was spoken; so shall your seed be. It is true Abraham was the forefather of the Israelites that came through his grandson Jacob, whose name was later changed to Israel. God chose Jacob in place of his twin brother Esau to continue with the promise made to Abraham. This is seen in the Book of Genesis 35:11;

11 And God said unto him, I am god almighty: be fruitful and multiply; a nation and a company of nations shall be of thee, and kings shall come out of thy loins.

It is true that Israel indeed turned out to be a great nation. After the death of Joseph, the Bible tells us that although in bondage in Egypt, the children of Israel were fruitful and increased abundantly. They multiplied, waxed exceedingly mighty and the land was filled with them. A new king arose in Egypt who did not know Joseph, but said to the people, "Come on, let us deal wisely with them; lest they multiply, and it come to pass, that, when there falleth out any war, they join also unto our enemies, and fight against us, and so get them up out of the land. Therefore they did set over them taskmasters to afflict them with their burdens. And they built for Pharaoh treasure cities, Pithom and Raamses. But the more they afflicted them, the more they multiplied and grew. And they were grieved because of the children of Israel." (Exodus 1:10-12).

Great kings came out of Israel centuries after they had come out from slavery in Egypt, like David and Solomon, in fulfilment of the promise in Genesis 35:11. God talks about physical things in the Bible when in fact He is alluding to spiritual things, for God is Spirit. When God told Father Abraham that he will be the father of many nations, He was not only referring to the physical nations that came out of Israel, but also the spiritual nations that will come out of Him to a greater extent of the truth. When a man becomes born again through confession and reflection, though it is a physical pronouncement, it is a spiritual act to unite with the spiritual body of Christ. Today, any man, irrespective of his race, colour and location around the globe, can become part of this glorious Body which is Christ, the King of kings. He is far greater than all the kings that ever reigned in Israel.

Notes and Reflections for Readers

How Do I Become A Child of God?

The burning question remains, 'How do we become grafted into the Body of Christ?' Below, I will explain three concepts that will help us understand this mystery:

1) **Become Born Again**
2) **Receive Jesus**
3) **Believe In Jesus Christ**

Become Born Again

Nicodemus, the Pharisee and Jewish religious leader who was illuminated by the glorious gospel of Jesus Christ, visited Jesus secretly in the night to question Him about salvation. Christ said to him, "I tell you the truth, no one can see the kingdom of God unless he is born again." (John 3:3). Nicodemus marveled at this response and asked Jesus how can one become born again when he is already old? Does he have to enter his mother's womb the second time to be born again?

Jesus Christ replied, "That which is born of the flesh is flesh; and that which is born of the Spirit is Spirit. Do not marvel that I said to you, 'You must be born again.' The wind blows where it wishes, and you hear its sound, but you do not know where it comes from or where it goes. So it is with everyone who is born of the Spirit." (John 3:5-8)

The first time a person is born, he inherits the sinful nature that stems from Adam's disobedience in the Garden of Eden. No one has to teach a child how to sin. He naturally follows his own wrong desires, leading to such sins as lying, stealing and hating. Rather than being a child of God, he is a child of disobedience and wrath.

"As for you, you were dead in your transgressions and sins, in which you used to live when you followed the ways of this world and of the ruler of the kingdom of the air, the spirit who is now at work in those who are disobedient. All of us also lived among them at one time, gratifying the cravings of our sinful nature and following its desires and thoughts. Like the rest, we were by nature objects of wrath." Thankfully, the passage continues, "But because of his great love for us, God, who is rich in mercy, made us alive with Christ even when we were dead in transgressions – It is by grace you have been saved." (Ephesians 2:1-5).

A man becomes born again through normal confession, with his mouth renouncing his old ways and denying his old self to accept Christ in his life. He pronounces Christ as Lord and Savior over his new self. He believes in his heart as we get from the Bible in Romans 10:9, "If thou shalt confess with thy mouth the Lord Jesus, and shalt believe in thine heart that God hath raised him from the dead, thou shalt be saved." For with the heart, man believes in righteousness and with the mouth, confession leads to salvation. Though it is a physical pronouncement, it is a spiritual act to unite ourselves to the spiritual Body of Christ.

Today, any person, irrespective of their gender, race, colour age, religion or whatever deplorable moral situation they find themselves in can become part of this glorious Body which is Christ, King of kings, far greater than all the kings that ever ruled. Every human being has been created in the image of God. As seen in the Book of Genesis, everyone has their place in the spiritual Body of Christ which is the home of refuge for all. This is the reason why Christ gave Himself up as a sacrifice, replacing the sacrifice of bulls and sheep in the Old, so that it may be done now in the New. Once and for all, our freedom is perfectly granted.

How are we made alive through Christ / born again / made a child of God? We must receive Jesus!

RECEIVE JESUS

"Yet to all who received him, to those who believed in his name, he gave the right to become children of God." (John 1:12). This passage clearly explains how to become God's children. We must receive Jesus by believing in Him. What must we believe about Jesus? First, we must recognise that Jesus is the eternal Son of God who became man. Born through the power of the Holy Spirit by the Virgin Mary, Jesus did not inherit Adam's sinful nature. Therefore, He is called the second Adam. While Adam's one disobedience brought the curse of sin upon the world, Christ's perfect life can cover our sinful ones. Our response must be to repent, turn away from sin and trust that His perfect life will purify us.

Secondly, we must have faith in Jesus Christ as Savior. God's plan was to sacrifice His perfect Son on the Cross to pay for the punishment we deserve for our sins – death. Christ's death frees those who receive Him from the power and penalty of sin.

Finally, we must follow Jesus as Lord. After raising Christ up as the victor over sin and death, God gave Him all authority. By God's grace granting us pardon and faith in the Savior, we are born again to new life as God's children. Only those who receive Jesus, not merely knowing about Him, but relying solely on Him for salvation, submitting to Him as Master, and loving Him as the supreme treasure, become God's children.

BELIEVE IN JESUS CHRIST

The bible says in Romans 10:9-19;

9 That if thou shalt confess with thy mouth the Lord Jesus, and shalt believe in thine heart that God hath raised him from the dead, thou shalt be saved.

10 For with the heart the man believeth unto righteousness; and with the mouth confession is made unto salvation.

Here, Paul talks about two important elements that work together to bring forth the salvation of the lost: 1) Believe in your heart. 2) Confess with your mouth. Both of them are essential and inseparable for man's salvation in this new era of grace, in which we as Christians should follow. I have already talked about confession leading to salvation which is the bold declaration of faith. You must renounce your old ways and take up your new identity, inviting Christ to be Lord and guide over your new self. The first, 'Believe in your heart,' will always lead to the second, 'Confess with your mouth,' for we can't rely on something we do not believe in. The Bible says in Matthew 7:21

The bible says in Mathew 7:21;

21 Not everyone that saith unto me, Lord, Lord, shall enter into the kingdom of heaven; but he that doeth the will of my father which is in heaven.

In the Book of John 6, Jesus had a confrontation with the unbelieving crowd. He told them not to labor for the meat that perishes, but for the meat that endures unto everlasting life. After some dispute with them, they finally asked Him what is the work of the Father; Jesus answered that the work of God is to believe in Him whom the Father has sent, Jesus Christ. Now we should acknowledge one thing that we Christians have refused to understand. This all happened in the era of the New. John was of the New, he was an Apostle of Jesus Christ and his gospel speaks about the will of God through Christ. Like most Christians say, as they hear their pastors say, the New Testament does not cancel the Old Testament. The new testament does not cancel the old yes of course but, in fact the New Testament fulfils the Old Testament perfectly well (Mathew 5:17). If we preach the truth, but conceal the greater truth from people, then our motives are based on false intentions. We hear Paul say in 1 Corinthians 7:39 that it is but legal that a woman is bound to her husband for as long as he lives. Only when he dies is she free from the laws holding her bound to her husband. Paul here was not talking about physical union between a man and woman, becoming husband and wife, bringing forth physical babies in the course of their living together, but he was talking about a spiritual union between the children of God and the law of old from which they are later on divorced and freed from, with the coming of Christ. Everything in the old, is but a shadow of the new. For example, in the old testament the Israelites were in bondage in Egypt and were later on delivered by the hand of Moses into the promised land Canaan. In the new testament, Christ who represent the land of Freedom (Canaan), comes to deliver us from the land of bondage, Egypt (the law), through grace, by the cross.

I believe the people in the Book of Matthew were sincere and no doubt religious. Let us hear their testimony in Matthew 7:22. "Many will say to me on that day, 'Lord, Lord, did we not prophesy in your name and in your name drive out demons and in your name perform many miracles?'" Sure, they did many wonderful things in Jesus' name, but listen to what Jesus responded in Matthew 7:23. "Then I will tell them plainly, 'I never knew you. Away from me, you evildoers!'" These people had spent their lives prophesying, casting out devils and doing many wonderful works all in Jesus' name. Only for Christ to tell them in the end to depart from Him, that they are workers of immorality and failed to do God's will. People get the wrong impression that they can earn their way to Heaven and merit salvation by their own works, but this is a lie. There is nothing we can do to earn Heaven.

The passage of Scripture we just read is perhaps the most eye-opening truth in the Bible. It is hard to imagine these sincere people being cast away by Christ, after spending so much time trying to help others in the name of Jesus. We learn a few truths from this passage:

Firstly, many false religions operate in Jesus' name. Matthew 7:23 says that false prophets are 'workers of iniquity.' A lot of Christians out there are bread, sign and wonders seeking Christians, like the crowd Jesus was addressing in the Book of John 6. If we seek Christ with the wrong intention in our hearts, we will receive Him the wrong way. Our whole knowledge about Him will be built on worthless foundation, and if a house is built on useless foundation, big trouble awaits the occupant of the house. Solomon, son of David, was blessed beyond measures because of his honorable intentions. What is your intention for seeking Christ, brethren?

Secondly, the only way to be saved is by doing God's will. What is God's will? We find the answer in John 6:40. "For my Father's will is that everyone who looks to the Son and believes in him shall have eternal life, and I will raise them up at the last day." God's will is for every person to see Jesus as He is portrayed in the Word of God and to trust Him. We must believe in Jesus Christ as He is presented in the Scriptures, God manifested in the flesh.

Thirdly, we are not all God's children. I often hear modernists say, "We are all God's children." Not so! We are all God's creation, but we are definitely not all God's children. A modernist is someone who speaks of spiritual matters, but is unsaved; they make light of the Bible. Only those who are truly born-again can truthfully claim to be the children of God. Concerning salvation, someone has foolishly taught that all rivers lead to the ocean. Actually, it all depends how you look at it and which path you choose to travel. It is frightening the way people think and base their eternal destiny on such foolish thinking. God inspired those who authored the Bible to show us the way to salvation, so we would not guess or make erroneous conclusions.

"For it is with your heart that you believe and are justified, and it is with your mouth that you profess your faith and are saved." (Romans 10:10). It is with the heart that we believe in the Lord in order to be saved. The confession of the mouth can only follow the believing of the heart. It is the trusting of the heart that makes us righteous in God's eyes, because of Christ's righteousness which is applied to our record. A believing heart is a greater prerequisite than a confessing mouth. Why? Because it is 'with the heart' that a person believes and considers righteousness. The very fact that a mute person cannot confess Christ audibly is proof that God does not require it as part of saving faith. Salvation is of the heart; we are saved by believing in Jesus Christ.

NOTES AND REFLECTIONS FOR READERS

IS WATER BAPTISM A PREREQUISITE FOR SALVATION?

Water baptism does not save nor is it required to be saved. "He that believeth and is baptized shall be saved; but he that believeth not shall be damned." (Mark 16:16). The emphasis is upon BELIEVING. Water baptism cannot save a person any more than walking into a garage makes you an automobile. A weeding ring means nothing if you have no marriage. Likewise, water baptism means little if you do not believe in the Lord with all your heart. Salvation is of the heart.

What does matter is that you BELIEVE in your HEART that Jesus is the Savior, the Son of God, and you trust upon Him and His blood sacrifice to wash away your sins. You do not need to open your mouth to be saved, salvation is of the heart. It is common these days to hear people claim that they used to be a Christian. That is not true, there is no such thing as a former Christian. They may have experienced the philosophy of Christianity or belonged to a religious organization, but they never became a born-again Christian in Jesus Christ. Many people today have Churchianity without Christianity. The world's churches are filled with religious people who are woefully ignorant of the truth of God's Word. Their minds have been filled with religious ideas and Biblical stories, but they have never personally come to God as a filthy, rotten and guilty sinner in need of salvation. It is only when we repent by admitting to God that we are vile sinners as He has declared us to be in His holy Word, and place our faith in the blood sacrifice of Jesus

Christ to wash away our sins, that we become regenerated and anew. We must believe that Jesus is the Christ, the Son of God. The Bible is clear that salvation is by grace through faith in Jesus Christ not by works of any kind (Ephesians 2:8-9). So, any interpretation which comes to the conclusion that baptism or any other act is necessary for salvation is a debatable interpretation.

It is important to note that nowhere in the passage of John 3:3-7 is baptism mentioned. While baptism is mentioned later in this chapter (John 3:22-30), that is in a different setting (Judea instead of Jerusalem) and at a different time from the discussion with Nicodemus. This is not to say that Nicodemus was unfamiliar with baptism, either from the Jewish practice of baptizing Gentile converts to Judaism or from John the Baptist's ministry. However, simply reading these verses in context would give one no reason to assume Jesus was speaking of baptism, unless one was looking to read into the passage a preconceived idea or theology. To automatically read baptism into this verse, simply because it mentions 'water' is unwarranted.

Those who believe baptism is required for salvation will point to "born of water" as evidence. As one person has put it, "Jesus describes it and tells him plainly to be born of water and Spirit. This is a perfect description of baptism! Jesus could not have given a more detailed and accurate explanation of baptism." However, if Jesus intended to say that one must be baptized to be saved, He clearly would have stated, "Truly, truly, I say to you, unless one is baptized and born of the Spirit, he cannot enter into the kingdom of God." Further, if Jesus had made such a statement, He would have contradicted numerous other Bible passages that make it clear that salvation is by faith (John 3:16, 3:36 and Ephesians 2:8-9). We should not lose sight of the fact that when Jesus was speaking to Nicodemus, the ordinance of Christian baptism was not yet in effect. This inconsistency of interpreting Scripture is seen when one asks those who believe baptism is required for salvation why the thief on the Cross did not need to be baptized to be saved. A common reply to that question is, "The thief on the Cross was still under the Old Covenant and therefore not subject to this baptism. He was saved just like anyone else under the Old Covenant." So, in essence, the same people who say the thief did not need to be baptized because he was "under the Old Covenant" will use John 3:5 as proof that baptism is necessary for salvation. They insist that Jesus is telling Nicodemus that he must be baptized to be saved even though he too was under the Old Covenant. If the thief on the Cross was saved without being baptized, why would Jesus tell Nicodemus that he needed to be baptized?

The second common interpretation of this passage and the one that best fits the overall context of the Bible is the one that sees the phrase "born of water and the Spirit" as 'born-again' or 'born from above.' When Jesus told Nicodemus that he must be "born of water and the Spirit," He was not referring to literal water (i.e. baptism or the amniotic fluid in the womb), but was referring to the need for spiritual cleansing and renewal. Throughout the Old Testament (Psalms 51:2, Ezekiel 36:25) and the New Testament (John 13:10, 15:3, 1 Corinthians 6:11, Hebrews 10:22), water is often used figuratively of spiritual cleansing that is brought forth by the Holy Spirit through the Word of God at the moment of salvation (Ephesians 5:26, Titus 3:5).

The Barclay Daily Study Bible describes this concept in this way: "There are two thoughts here. Water is the symbol of cleansing. When Jesus takes possession of our lives and when we love Him with all our hearts, the sins of the past are forgiven and forgotten. The Spirit is the symbol of power. When Jesus takes possession of our lives, it is not only that the past is forgiven and forgotten. If that were all, we might as well proceed to make the same mess all over again; but into life there enters a new power which enables us to be what by ourselves we could never be, and to do what by ourselves we could never do. Water and the Spirit stand for the cleansing and the strengthening power of Christ which wipes out the past and gives victory in the future."

Therefore, the 'water' mentioned in this verse is not literal physical water but rather the 'living water' Jesus promised the woman at the well in John 4:10 and the people in Jerusalem in John 7:37-39. It is the inward purification and renewal produced by the Holy Spirit that brings forth spiritual life to a dead sinner. Jesus reinforces this truth in John 3:7-8 when He restates that one must be born again and that this newness of life can only be produced by the Holy Spirit.

Jesus rebukes Nicodemus in John 3:10 by asking him, "Are you the teacher of Israel, and do not understand these things?" What is it that Nicodemus, a teacher of the Old Testament, should have known and understood? It is that God had promised in the Old Testament a time was coming in which He would "sprinkle clean water on you, and you will be clean; I will cleanse you from all your filthiness and from all your idols. Moreover, I will give you a new heart and put a new Spirit within you; and I will remove the heart of stone from your flesh and give you a heart of flesh. I will put My Spirit within you and cause you to walk in My statutes, and you will be careful to observe My ordinances." (Ezekiel 36:25-27). Jesus rebuked Nicodemus because he failed to recall one of the key Old Testament passages pertaining to the New Covenant (Jeremiah 31:33). Nicodemus should have been expecting this. Why would Jesus rebuke Nicodemus for not understanding baptism when baptism is nowhere mentioned in the Old Testament?

While this verse does not teach baptism is required for salvation, we should be careful not to neglect the importance of baptism. The practice of baptism is the symbol for what takes place when one is born-again. Although it does not save us, baptism's importance should not be downplayed or minimized. What saves us is the cleansing work of the Holy Spirit when we are regenerated by the Holy Spirit (Titus 3:5).

Christian baptism is the means by which a person makes a public profession of faith and discipleship. In the waters of baptism, a person says wordlessly, "I confess faith in Christ; Jesus has cleansed my soul from sin, and I now have a new life of sanctification." Christian baptism illustrates in dramatic style the death, burial, and resurrection of Christ. At the same time, it also illustrates our death to sin and new life in Christ. As the sinner confesses Lord Jesus as Savior, he dies to sin and is raised to a brand new life. Being submerged in the water represents death to sin, and emerging from the water represents the cleansed holy life that follows salvation.

Romans 6:4

4 Therefore we are buried with him by baptism into death: that like Christ was raised up from the dead by the glory of the Father, even so we also should walk in newness of life.

Very simply, baptism is an outward testimony of the inward change in a believer's life. Christian baptism is an act of obedience to the Lord after salvation. Although baptism is closely associated with salvation, it is not a requirement to be saved. The Bible shows the order of events:

1) A person believes in the Lord Jesus
2) He is baptized

This sequence is seen in Acts 2:41. "Those who accepted Peter's message were baptized" (see also Acts 16:14-15). A new believer in Jesus Christ should desire to be baptized as soon as possible. In Acts 8, Philip speaks the good news about Jesus to the Ethiopian eunuch, and as they traveled along the road, they came to some water and the eunuch said, "Look, here is water. What can stand in the way of my being baptized?" Right away, they stopped the chariot and Philip baptized the man. Baptism illustrates a believer's identification with Christ's birth, death and resurrection. Everywhere the gospel is preached, people are to be baptized.

NOTES AND REFLECTIONS FOR READERS

NOTES AND REFLECTIONS FOR READERS

THE TRUE BODY AND BLOOD OF JESUS

This is one of the key issues that my book, *The Great Outcry*, seeks to address, so I will do my best to put forward the facts in a straight, subtle, friendly and firm way where necessary, as I seek to reach as many Souls as I can with this awareness, bringing out the silent, invisible, heartbroken man within me. My desire is not to convince any man to listen to these truths, but I make my petitions with the Great I AM, for even though He has put in me this Spirit that troubles greatly, let Him in the same manner rain down the Spirit of conviction upon every heart that receives these words. If He causes rain to fall upon the seeds sown by the sower who after sowing goes to his resting place, then surely God will cause it to rain upon His sowed seed that they may sprout and bring forth worthy fruits in due season.

I will use the Catholic Church and its sacrament of the Holy Eucharist as an example, because it is the oldest religious denomination after Christ.

WHAT IS THE SACRAMENT OF THE HOLY EUCHARIST?

The catholic church has attached so much importance to a lot of traditions and rites that have no place in the kingdom of God and the salvation of man, one of which is the sacrament of the holy eucharist. The catholic church has made the people to believe that the sacrament conveys grace to anyone who receives it **worthily**, and that it makes present the Christ's sacrifice on the cross and for this reason, it is known as the holy sacrifice of the mass. They profess that upon consecration, the bread and wine changes completely into the actual body and blood, of Christ, known as transubstantiation; the bread and wine used in the Sacrament of the Holy Eucharist become, not merely a sign, but in actual reality the Body and Blood of Christ, and by the taking of it, forgiveness of sins and food for the spirit is obtained. The catholic church teaches that the manner in which the change occurs is a mystery: "The signs of bread and wine become, in a way surpassing understanding, the Body and Blood of Christ."

The Catholics believe receiving the Holy Communion honorably brings us graces that affect us spiritually and physically. Spiritually, our spirit become more united with Christ through the grace we receive and through the change in our actions that those graces effect. Catholics believe that frequent Communion increases our love for God and for our neighbor, and relieves us from our passions. Priests and spiritual directors who counsel people struggling with passions, especially sexual sins, often urge frequent reception not only of the Sacrament of Confession but of the Sacrament of Holy Communion. By receiving Christ's Body and Blood, our own bodies are sanctified and we grow in our likeness to Christ. As Fr. John Hardon points out in his *Modern Catholic Dictionary*, the Church teaches that "A final effect of Communion is to remove the personal guilt of venial sins, and the temporal punishment (earthly and purgatorial) due to forgiven sins, whether venial or mortal."

To better grasp the spiritual meaning of the allegorical bread and wine Jesus spoke about, I would like to critically examine the Book of John 6 and Mark 14. John 6 opens up with the fact that Jesus went over the Sea of Galilee, also known as Lake Tiberias, and a great multitude followed Him because they saw the miracles He had performed on the diseased. The Jewish festival of Passover was approaching. Jesus went up to a mountain and sat with His disciples. When Jesus raised His eyes and saw a great company approach Him, he asked Philip, "Whence shall we buy bread, that these may eat?"

Philip replied, "Two hundred pennyworth of bread is not sufficient for them, that every one of them may take a little."

One of His disciples, Andrew, Simon Peter's brother, said, "There is a lad here, which hath five barley loaves, and two small fishes: but what are they among so many?"

Jesus replied, "Make the men sit down." There was plenty of grass to sit on, thus about five thousand people joined them. Jesus took the loaves, gave thanks and distributed them to the disciples who then shared the bread with those seated on the grass. Plenty of fish were shared around too.

When they ate plenty, Jesus said to His disciples, "Gather up the fragments that remain, that nothing be lost." They filled twelve baskets with the fragments of the five barley loaves which remained over and above unto them that had eaten.

The men who had seen Jesus perform these miracles, feeding five thousand people with just five loaves of bread and two fish went out the following day seeking Him. They wanted to make Jesus King by force, so they searched the land and sea until it was getting dark, but they did not find Him. When they finally located Jesus, they asked Him where He was from. Immediately discerning their hearts, Jesus told them that they seek Him not for the miracles He performed or His words of truth, but for the fact that they needed bread to fill their stomachs. Jesus was revealing the hidden mystery, the secret truth that they should labor not for the meat that perishes, but for the meat which endures unto everlasting life which the Son of Man shall give unto them. At this stage, Jesus had not yet been crucified on the Cross and the intended meat (spiritual) had not yet been ready for consumption. Also the work of the Father (in this era) is to believe in Him (Christ) whom God had sent, but their minds were on their physical bellies.

Our fathers did eat manna in the desert; as it is written, He gave them bread from Heaven to eat. Jesus replied, "Verily, verily, I say unto you, Moses gave you not that bread from heaven; but my Father giveth you the true bread from heaven. For the bread of God is he which cometh down from heaven, and giveth life unto the world."

Then they said, "Lord, evermore give us this bread."

Jesus continued, "I am the bread of life: he that cometh to me shall never hunger; and he that believeth on me shall never thirst." Jesus was revealing great truth, but their spiritual ears were sealed with the hunger for physical bread and meat.

Jesus Christ persisted even more, speaking in parables. "I am that bread of life. Your fathers did eat manna in the wilderness, and are dead. This is the bread which cometh down from heaven, that a man may eat thereof, and not die. I am the living bread which came down from heaven: if any man eat of this bread, he shall live for ever: and the bread that I will give is my flesh, which I will give for the life of the world." (John 6:48-51).

These things were taught in the Synagogue in Capernaum. Jesus Christ who is Spirit was talking about spiritual bread here, the invisible bread that cannot be seen with the physical eyes. Jesus told the crowd that their fathers ate manna during the time of Moses, physical bread that went into their physical bodies which perished years later. Jesus, here, was talking about spiritual bread which goes on to feed the invisible spiritual man within us. In the person of Christ, He comes into our Spirits to dwell there forever. The moment we become born again, declaring Him as Lord and Savior of our lives, He abides in the spirit of every born again Christian. As the physical body hungers for physical food, so too does Christ who lives in our spiritual body. We are one with Christ, for we are joined together in one body, Him being the Head of the body. The question remains, what spiritual food does Christ desire so that He may grow to maturity within us and we may increase in the spiritual awareness of who we truly are? The spiritual food is the Word of God. I am not talking about the head knowledge we get when we read the physical words of the Bible, but I am referring to the revelation of the hidden mystery, which is the wisdom of God, kept very far from the understanding of the carnal senses we receive when we read the Word of God, this is what Peter, Paul, John and all the other apostles had which was highly opposed to the head knowledge of the law which the highly educated Pharisees and Sadducees who rejected Christ as the Messiah had. That hidden wisdom is given by the Spirit of

God. Let's take a banana fruit as an example. It is not the yellow peeling that nourishes our bodies, but the white fruit covered by the peeling.

John 1:1-14

1 In the beginning was the word, the word was with God and the word was God

2 The same was in the beginning with God.

3 All things were made by him; and without him was not anything made that was made.

4 In him was life; and the life was the light of men.

5And the light shineth in darkness; and darkness comprehended it not.

6 There was a man sent from God whose name was John.

7 The same came for a witness, to bear witness of the light, that all men through him might believe.

8 He was not that light, but was sent to bear withess of that light.

9 That was the true Light, whichlighteth every man that cometh into the world.

10 He was in the world, and the world was made by him, and the world knew him not.

11 he came to his own, and his own received him not.

12 But as many as receive him, to them, gave he the power to become the sons of God, even to them that believe on his name.

13 Which were born, not of blood, nor of the will of the flesh, nor of the will of man, but of God.

14 And the word was made flesh, and dwelt among us, (and we beheld his glory, the glory as of the only begotten of the father), full of grace and truth

In these verses, we are told that in the beginning was the Word, the Word was with God and the Word was God. You may wonder what this means. God is Spirit; we can't see spoken words with our physical eyes nor can we see God with our physical eyes.

John 6:60-64

60 Many therefore of his disciples, when they had heard this, said this is an hard saying; who can hear it?

61 When Jesus knew in himself that his disciples murmured at it, he said unto them, Doth this offend you?

62 What and if ye shall see the son of man ascend up where he was before?

63 It is the spirit that quickenth; the flesh profiteth nothing: the words that I speak unto you, they are spirit and they are life.

64 But there are some of you that believe not. For Jesus knew from the beginning who they were that believed not, and who should betray him.

Everything is clear here. Jesus tells His disciples that it is the Spirit that has life, the flesh profits nothing. In other words, it is not only the physical bread that we break in our Churches that will revive our Soul, but also the Word (the spiritual bread) that holds Spirit and life. It is the Word which the Spirit reveals to us that is of importance; that truth can also be obtained through the writings in the Holy Bible.

Luke 22: 19-20

19 And he took bread, and gave thanks, and brake it, and gave unto them, saying, this is my body which is given for you this do in remembrance of me.

20 Likewise, also the cup after supper, saying this is the new testament in my blood, which is shed for you.

Jesus told His disciples in verse 19 that they should break bread and do this often in remembrance of Him. Parishioners go about breaking bread and drinking wine weekly, some even daily. Let me ask you this question, can that physical bread and wine give someone, who has virtually no knowledge of the Word of God or anything about Christ and His death on the Cross, more knowledge? No. That which can make us remember these things and our position in Christ are the spiritual bread and wine. This alone can take us back to the position in which we were before the fall.

1 Corinthians 10 : 16- 17

16 The cup of blessing which we bless, is it not the communion of the blood of Christ ?

17 For we being many are one bread, and one body, for we are all partakers of that one bread.

The word communion means unity or sharing of thoughts and emotions; intimate communication when we share the Word of God together. We partake of His Holy Communion which all Christians are a part of. As Paul says, "For we being many are one bread, and one body: for we are all partakers of that one bread." The drinking or partaking of His Blood consists of believing that the Blood which He shared on the Cross for our sins is sufficient and able to save us from our sins.

Some years ago, I stopped reading my Bible for a few months. Soon after, I had a dream of Our Lord. He directed me to get back into the ritual of reading the Bible. The dream went like this. I was one of two servants; one was a cook and I was an errand man. Our Master, a great man, was very fond of me. One day, the Master sat on the dining table and asked for His food. He was dressed in white and His face was shiny like the sun. The cook served him all kinds of food delicacies, but He refused to eat, so the cook did not know what else to do. He called me to attend to the Master for he knew the Master was closer to me. When I went to Him, I said, "Master, you said you are hungry, so the cook tells me, but there on your table are all kinds of delicious meals that you won't eat. What then do you desire to eat? Tell me and I will promptly prepare it for you."

He raised His head and looked straight at me. His eyes were red, he shook His head several times from left to right then said, "This is not my food, give me my food." When He said this, I immediately awoke from sleep and I understood that He was telling me to go back to studying the Word. That way, I (He) would be nourished spiritually. He did not ask me to go and eat the physical bread and wine, but to read the Word day and night, and meditate on it.

Brothers, let your heart and desires be on the Lord God Almighty. Assume you are a father and have two sons. One only comes to you when he needs one thing or another, while his brother comes to you to find out what you need. Which one of them will gain your respect and secrets?

Jesus knows our every move and motives. He meets our needs and desires according to our motives. What is your motive for seeking God? Is it for your belly, self-gratification, to make a big name for yourself so people will salute you or is it to find comfort, love, wisdom and truth from the greatest teacher of modern times, the greatest miracle worker and the rock? Look good people of God, true greatness is in knowing the truth which is the light of God. This will reflect the love of God and cause a man to reach out to humanity with a true and loving heart. You can't expect a good man's perception of truth and light to be clouded by darkness and evil. It does not work like that. We will never hail a Pharisee nor can we even remember their names, but the name Christ, Paul, John the Baptist, etc. have been written on giant walls with God's own Hand. They are meant to be there permanently from generation to generation and from ages to ages. These are great men in the Godly and true sense of the term. These men did not parade and seek greatness, but they pressed hard to propagate the truth. In return, God decorated them with true greatness which was not their original desires but their merits. Many people from that era used their free will to hate these people because their mind was unwilling to compromise, but they had no ability to stop God's Hand of favor upon their lives. Some people seek God because they want to make money, build mansions, own private jets, fulfil their unsatisfying lustful carnal desires or become the super boss within their community, all while still wanting to have fast and easy access to the ends of the earth.

Throughout Europe, it is rare to find a man of God whose heart aches for the will of God, loves God with His whole being or hurts when he sees the lost drowning. I am yet to meet someone who is ready to give his whole life for Jesus. Why not, why can't we do this for someone so dear as Him when we know full well the things He has done for us? Is our knowledge of Him so basic that we do not comprehend these things? Do we lack warmth within our hearts? Have we let materialism replace the love of God within us? We should know that these things are vain, and one day we will all die and leave them behind. No one who leaves this world takes anything with him. You can't worship God and your possessions, and expect to be focused and on the right path. The crowd that went after Jesus for the sake of their bellies did not understand Him or His message which was wrapped up in mystery. So too will you never grasp the mystery of Heaven until your heart is renewed. Until you make an outcry like David for a heart of flesh, the love of God can't dwell within you. Stop counting money when you see members in your church and start embracing the lost sheep of God who need to be saved. Nurture them in the true wisdom of Christ and let the love of God burn within your spirit, otherwise your work is worthless. Woe to those who hold power, but use it for people's downfall. Brethren, the love of God is the principal key. The Bible says in 1 John 4:8, "He that loveth not knoweth not God; for God is love." In 1 John 4:16, the Bible says, "And we have known and believed the love that God hath to us. God is love; and he that dwelleth in love dwelleth in God, and God in him."

Brethren, I did not put these verses in the Bible, John did. He lived with Christ and passionately followed Him everywhere He went, so that he could record that glorious wisdom as it was given to him by the Spirit. God's truth, wisdom and love are granted to us, not by professors of theology or any man outside of us, but the One that is inside holds the key. Go to the Man inside. On his dying bed, Great John Wesley's father revealed to him this secret that fellowship with the Man inside is proof of Christianity. The Man of the Spirit lives within you, so please go to Him.

I recall wandering in Tiko, my home town, searching for food and a place to sleep. God persistently called me in dreams, visions and through other great men of God. Brother Mike was one of such men who inspired me to follow the path of ministry. During this time in my life, I had no money to pay for my school of ministry fees. I relied on God to open a door and lead me to a destiny helper who would pay my fees or grant me a scholarship abroad. I applied to about five schools abroad, but I was particularly interested in one. It was the Midwestern State University in the United States of America. My friend, Esapa Javis, recommended that school as we could apply for a scholarship. We prayed and fasted for God's intervention, but we were not granted admission because we could not afford the tuition fees. Before we were refused admission, I had a dream that we were refused admission in the school, but the Associate Director of the school, Kerrie Cale, called me privately and gave me some documents and a precious perfume. I did not know the meaning of the dream or what God was trying to say. I prayed to no avail; God did not give me the interpretation. I contacted Madam Cale hoping maybe she had some good news for me, but no, all they required from me was the running cost of the course and nothing more. They were not interested in me, my dream or whatever story I had to tell. I struggled to understand the meaning of the dream from God, to no avail, so I finally gave up.

One or two years later, I received a revelation from God saying He has seen all my struggles and endeavors to travel that I should go on foot, to the way of the North of Africa, for the way was clear, so I maneuvered my way to Italy through the Sahara desert. I persistently asked God to open a door for me to get accepted into a school of ministry, even while still in a refugee camp in Milan, for I still had no single penny to my name. I applied at schools in Europe and America, like the Oral Roberts, but I was refused admission for lack of money. I even travelled to Rotterdam in Holland with twenty euros which I used to buy the train ticket. I went in person to the Fire School of Ministry, pleading with the director to please hear me out and consider me, but he turned me down sharply saying that it was a new school and they desperately needed funds for running costs. A student, Johannes Deelstra, drove me to the station with his wife, took me to McDonalds and bought me a burger to fill my crying stomach. He even paid for my train back to Belgium. Brother Johannes and his wife Jiska had pity on me, but they could do little to help me out, yet God was still showing me marvelous things He desired to accomplish through me.

One day, after giving up searching for a bible school and God's miracle, I had a dream that changed my life and gave me deep understanding concerning God and the path I was to walk. Through it, I could understand what God was telling me in my previous dream back in Tiko, my home town. I have had countless dreams of me flying, but this one was different. In the dream, I saw myself moving with some friends to a school and my Spirit Man was giving me the understanding that we were going to a Bible school. All of a sudden, I saw the Holy Spirit pass by and sweep me off my feet. We flew together then He dropped me into a classroom. There was no teacher in the classroom, just me alone in front of a big screen and DVD player. In my hand was my white Bible (the King James version) and a DVD. I went to the front of the class and played my DVD. It was the Word of God inspiring me to behold the Man within. From that day on, I rested from searching. My key prayer topic shifted from "Let God grant me free access into a Bible school" to "Let Him give me more knowledge, wisdom and insight from within," for He is indeed the spring of living water. It is the hidden mystery in His Word that is revealed by the Spirit alone. Paul says it all in 1 Corinthians 2:5-14

1 Corinthians 2 :5-14

5 That your faith should not stand in the wisdom of men, but in the power of God.

6 Howbeit we speak wisdom among them that are perfect : yet not the wisdom of this world, nor of the princes of this world, that come to nought.

7 But we speak the wisdom of God in a mystery, even the hidden wisdom, which God ordained before the world unto our glory.

8 Which none of the princes of this world knew, for had they known it, they would not have crucified the Lord of glory.

9 But as it is written, Eye has not seen nor ear heard neither have entered into the heart of man, the things which God hath prepared for them that love him.

10 But God hath revealed them unto us by his spirit, for the spirit searcheth all things, yea, the deep things of God.

11 For what man knoweth, the things of a man save the spirit of man which is in him? Even so the things of God knoweth no man, but the spirit of God.

12 Now we have received, not the spirit of this world, but the spirit which is of God; that we might know the things which are freely given to us by God.

13 Which things also we speak, not in the words which man's wisdom teacheth, but which the Holy Ghost teacheth; comparing spiritual things with spiritual.

14 But the natural man receieth not the things of the spirit of God, for they are foolishness unto him neither can he know them, because they are spiritually discerned.

Brethren, I pray that you allow your prayer topic to shift from breakthrough, breakthrough, breakthrough to "God, let me know you more, let me love you more, I want to know your purpose in my life, and may you accomplish it through me." Beloved, I tell you that everything you yearn for is in these prayer topics that will be revealed to you in due season. No need for struggles, you just need to accept the power and validity of the truth, to die, be buried and wake up in the reality of He, Christ who called you unto this victory, gloriously from age to age, unto the dawn of noonday I pray that my writing will strengthen a brother who feels rejected, desolate and alone, so that his tears will turn into joy at the fact that God has a plan and purpose for his or her life. At one point in my life, in Belgium, I found myself crying tears of pain, for life was showing me a difficult and uncertain path, I worked so hard but had nothing, it was like all doors were shot on me, wheras my friends were making it big, and would make fun of me from time to time. God came to me in a dream and told me to stop crying and focus on what I have, for that which He has given me He has given to no one else. That is the way it is; God has given every one of His children unique abilities, and until you discover your own, your life will be sorrowful and unfulfilling. God knows our every needs and desires, and is very timely to meet up with them. Only He does not operate as man does; good things happen in His destined and appointed time. God told the Israelites on their way to the promise land that He will lead them safely and that He will send hornets before them to drive their enemies away, the Hivites and the Canaanites. He will not drive them out in one year, lest the land will become desolate and the beast of the field will multiply against them, but little by little, He will drive them out until the Israelites increase and inherit the land (Exodus 23:20-30). This is how God guards His children and operates the great things. He reveals everything to them in bits, so that they increase in the knowledge and power of Him, and become fully refined to handle that which He has reserved ahead for them. Only they need to be patient and wait on God's time; this I am talking from experience. Mathew 6:33 says;

33 But seek ye first the kingdom of God and his righteousness; and all other things shall be added unto you.

Many Churches, today, before the sharing of the physical bread and wine, assumed to be the body and blood of Jesus Christ, say something like this. If you know in your heart that you are clean and worthy to partake of the Body and Blood of Christ, please come forth. If you know you are worthy! We are saved by the finished works of Christ on the Cross. That is final. The conditional 'if' clause in front of the question impels a doubt. The church members start to examine themselves, scanning their minds to acknowledge their sins and whether they are truly worthy. This is nothing but confusion. Can we partake in a worthy manner? Yes, absolutely! Can even the best of us, of our own abilities be truly worthy to eat of the Lord's Body and drink of His Blood? No, absolutely not! To claim that we are worthy is putting a vast amount of confidence in the flesh and our ability to free ourselves of sin. It is a prideful and self-righteous assumption. No one is truly worthy to partake in Our Lord's Body and Blood, and if we are to be worthy, it would only be through the Body and Blood of Christ making us worthy. If we don't partake in it, then how are we supposed to become worthy? That is like telling somebody to wash themselves before they are worthy to take a bath.

To say that we must rid ourselves of sin before we can partake is to read something into Scripture that was never said. To tell God's people that they will drink judgment unto themselves if they have any form of sin in their hearts as they symbolically remember what Christ did for them is spiritual abuse. Such a belief drives people away from wanting to partake at all.

If we are to examine our hearts for sin, what are we looking for? Little sins like lust and anger or the big ones like living in adultery? Are you going to honestly tell me that your heart is sinless every time you receive Holy Communion? Have you really obtained that achievement here on earth? Or are the little sins forgivable, but the big ones must be dealt with? Must we be fully unaware of any sin in our lives, including our thoughts and feelings, before we can partake in the Body and Blood of Christ in remembrance of what Jesus did for us? If we need to deal with sin in our hearts, then that includes the seemingly invisible ones, such as fear, unbelief, ingratitude, etc. When we take sin to that level at God's holy standard, then even the best of us will fall short.

Let us take the brand new believer who has numerous issues in their life that will take God years to work through them, not because He is powerless, but because He has given us free will. Should they go for years without receiving Holy Communion because there is sin within that has not been uprooted yet? Should we tell them that until they are worthy and have arrived at a place where they are aware of no sin in their heart, only then should they partake? If we tell them that and take Holy Communion before them, then we are claiming that we are right before God, and we are worthy to drink the Blood and eat the Body of Christ. I personally believe that such a position is to proclaim self-righteousness! Scripture is clear that everyone who believes upon Jesus is made righteous. Therefore, all who place their faith in Christ are worthy to partake.

When we first experienced salvation, and partook in His Body and Blood that was shed for us, were we worthy? Of course not! We were anything but worthy. If we were not worthy then, what makes us worthy today? This brings me to another theory that floats around the Church today. We start out in the Spirit, placing our faith in Christ to make us righteous, but then we start relying on our own ability to keep the law in order to maintain our righteousness. This was happening in the early Church and Paul rebuked them for it (Galatians 3:1-3). In the same way that we accepted Jesus into our hearts, and shared in His Body and Blood, we must also do this today in remembrance of what He did for us. Through faith, we come to Him as we are to relive what He has done for us; even if our place of need includes a struggle or bondage to sin in some area of our life.

If most of us examine our hearts looking for sin, we will surely find it somewhere, and it will disqualify us from wanting anything to do with partaking in the Body and Blood of Christ. Who in their right mind wants to bring condemnation unto themselves? How can you be sure that you have removed all sin from your heart? What is the difference between a small sin, such as envy, and a big sin, such as fornication? Sin is sin, and if we must make ourselves worthy by eliminating all sin, then we best remove every last drop and stand before the Lord in absolute perfection. I am not kidding! Either every sin is out of our hearts or it isn't. Even Paul admits that there was evil present in him even as a believer in Christ (Romans 7:21). We need to stand strong and be on guard to conquer this daily battle.

NOTES AND REFLECTIONS FOR READERS

TITHES

*T*he Great Outcry seeks to address this crucial subject for the fact that it has been burdening my Spirit and weighing me down. It troubles me that some supposed men of God have been misrepresenting this subject with malicious intentions of robbing their church members, to gain wealth. In the Book of John 12:6, John said this about Judas Iscariot. "This he said, not that he cared for the poor; but because he was a thief, and had the bag, and bare what was put therein."

Judas cared about the poor, not because he desired to see their lives get better, an armed robber, who helped himself from the money he was keeping. In a similar manner, many preachers nowadays capitalize on vain things of the Old such as tithes most especially, and will do everything they can to secure its payment by their church members. They have set aside the core things that matter in the kingdom of God, such as faith, love and grace which is our inheritance in Christ, and have focused on ego and greed. I would like to quote a key verse that is closely associated to this subject matter, Malachi 3:8-12

8 Will a man rob God? Yet ye have robbed me. But ye say, wherein have we robbed thee? In tithes and offerings.

9 Ye are cursed with a curse: for ye have robbed me, even this whole nation.

10 Bring ye all the tithes into the storehouse, that there may be meat in mine house, and prove me now here with, saith the lord of host, if I will not open you the windows of heaven, and pour out you out a blessing, that there shall not be room enough to receive it.

11 And I will rebuke the devourer for your sakes, and he shall not destroy the fruits of your ground; neither shall your vine cast her fruit before the time in the field, saith the Lord of hosts.

12 And all nations shall call you blessed: for ye shall be a delightsome land, saith the Lord of hosts.

I would now like to quote Matthew 5:17
Mathew 5:17
17 Think not that I am come to destroy the law, or the the prophets; I am not come to destroy the law but to fulfill it.

We see here in the words of Christ himself that He did not come to destroy the law of the prophets, but to fulfil it. For those who are unfamiliar with the term 'fulfil,' my dictionary provides four satisfactory definitions:

1) To bring about the completion or achievement of (a desire, promise, etc.)
2) To carry out or execute (a request, etc.)
3) To conform with or satisfy (regulations, demands, etc.)
4) To finish or reach the end (eg. He fulfilled his prison sentence).

Now that we understand the meaning of the term 'fulfil,' it is wise to examine Malachi 3:8-12. We should know that Malachi is the last Book of the Old Testament. It constitutes an article with the laws of the Old Testament which Christ came to fulfil in the New. If something has been fulfilled, it simply means its demands have been met. Any extra effort to fulfil demands that have already been met is useless.

In Malachi 3:10-12, the people had an obligation to bring tithe, in return, God would open up the windows of Heaven and pour out more blessings than the room can receive. The Lord promised to protect them, so all nations would call them blessed. In the Old, the people's blessings were conditioned upon tithing. It is important for us to get a clear understanding of what tithe is.

Tithe was an article of the law given by God unto Aaron and the children of Levi during the era of Moses, for the fact that they had no inheritance in the land at the time. They were assigned by God to collect a tenth of the people's land crops production and keep it in a place assigned by God, and were given specific instructions from God on how the tithes were to be used. They were obliged to sacrifice a tenth of the total of tithe received to Him; use part of it to sustain the orphans, fatherless, widows and strangers in the land. This tithing principle, which was an ordinance given unto the priests, was meant to sustain these ordained priests until the coming of Christ who is the greater High Priest. Jesus the long appointed high priest, was appointed by an oath like unto Melchizedek, and we who are of this new era of grace joined with Him in the priesthood.

Revelation 1:5-6

5 And from Jesus Christ, who is the faithful witness, and the first begotten of the dead, and the prince of the kings of the earth. Unto him that loves us, and washed us from our sins in his own blood,

6 And hath made us kings and priests unto God and his Father, to him be glory and dominion for ever and ever.

Amen.

The meaning of this truth that we have become joint priests with Christ is that Christ who has already atoned for our sins, has liberated us from the law, which made only a lineage of people, the Levites priests and high priests. Christ by this very act has replace the law of old with grace, through the cross which uplifted every man young and old, poor or rich, black or white into the position of priesthood, though, though some people cunningly are trying to have a monopoly over this position, do not expect them to tell you that is what they are trying to do, be wise and vigilant.

Some of us are really ignorant as to the power and glory we possess in this position that Christ has lifted us into which prosperity doctrine teachers wont dare to tell you or make you aware of, but I will in a few lines try to make you understand. Look brothers and sisters to begin with any man who calls himself a prosperity teacher, just that name prosperity teacher is a false man, that should be at the back of your mind. Coming back to our subject matter, a high priest was the supreme religious leader in the era of the old, a position that was hereditary and confined to one family line only, (Numbers 18:7). He alone had to offer a sin offering for his sins and for the sins of the rest of the people. Only the high priest was allowed to enter the most holy place of the temple to perform the service of atonement of sins which was at the tenth day of the month every year (Exodus 30:10).

You see brothers and sisters how God centered powers around the high priest, that not even Moses had assess into the hollies of hollies but we today have been given assess to this power house of God through Christ. The hollies of hollies being today not a physical innermost place in temple but the invisible temple that is in the spirit of every man that becomes anew in Christ, where Christ dwells.

He, Christ has set us free from the attacks of the enemy in every area of our lives. Our obligation is simply to accept the truth and believe. By growing in the knowledge of this truth, it becomes more real to us. This means that even if someone obliges us to pay tithes, in this glorious era of grace which we are privileged to live in, we should oblige him to pay first to us, because we are high priest, and equal living in the New. Why therefore will I pay tithes to him, why? why don't he pay to me rather ? The hollies of hollies, judging from its name, was a sacred room, a place no ordinary person could enter unless he was a high priest in the era of Moses and Joshua. It was God's special dwelling place in the midst of His people. Likewise our Spirits, the new era hollies of hollies which is accessible by none, not even the devil whose limitation is the soul, but the Prince of peace himself, the most high man. During their wandering in the wilderness, God appeared to the Israelites as a pillar of cloud or fire in and above the Holy of Holies.

A thick curtain separated the Holy of Holies from the Holy Place. The word 'veil' in Hebrew means a screen, divider or separator that hides. The curtain was shielding a holy God from sinful man. Whoever entered was entering the presence of God. In fact, anyone except the high priest who entered the Holy of Holies would die. Even the high priest, God's chosen mediator with His people, could only pass through the veil and enter this sacred dwelling (the power chamber) once a year, on a prescribed day called the Day of Atonement. When Christ died for us on the Cross, symbolically the curtain was split into two, meaning everyone now who becomes a joint high priest with Christ through confession has free access into the Holy of Holies.

Hebrews 10:19-22 says, "Therefore, brothers, since we have confidence to enter the Most Holy Place by the blood of Jesus, by a new and living way opened for us through the curtain, that is, his body... Let us draw near to God with a sincere heart in full assurance of faith."

Below are biblical passages that carefully speak of the introduction of tithing, how it was applied and its end.

Hebrews 6:20

20 Whither the forerunner is for us entered, even as Jesus made us high priests for ever after the order of Melchisedek.

Hebrews 7:1-10

1 For this Melchisedek, king of Salem, priest of the most high God, who met Abraham returning from the slaughter of the kings, and blessed him;

2 To whom also Abraham gave a tenth part of all first being by interpretation king of righteousness, and after that also king of Salem, which is king of peace;

3 Without father, without mother, without descent, having neither beginning of days, nor end of life; but made like unto the son of God; abideth a priest continually.

4 Now consider how great this man was, unto whom even the patriarch Abraham gave the tenth of the spoils.

5 And verily they that are of the sons of Levi who receive the office of priesthood, have a commandment to take tithes of the people according to the law, that is, of their brethren though they come out of the loins of Abraham.

6 But he whose descent is not counted from them received tithes from Abraham and blessed him that had the promise.

7 And without all contradictions the less is blessed of the better.

8 And here, men that die receive tithes; but there he receiveth them, of whom it is witnessed that he liveth.

9 And as I may say so, Levi also who receiveth tithes payed tithes in Abraham.

10 For he was yet in the loins of his father, when Melchisedec met him.

Many preachers will quote Hebrews 6:20 and try to justify themselves. They will say that Jesus Christ, our high priest, was made unto the order of Melchizedek, and Melchizedek received tithes, therefore them receiving tithes is justifiable. No brethren, we have no account in the whole of the New Testament of Jesus ever receiving a dime of tithe from anyone as Melchizedek did. The Hebrew word 'Melek' means king and 'tsedek' means righteousness, so his name means 'King of righteousness.' Since shalom means peace, he was also the 'king of peace.' These titles are significant because Melchizedek prefigures Jesus Christ.

We are told that Melchizedek was "without father or mother, without genealogy, without beginning of days or end of life. Like the Son of God, he remains a priest forever." From the grammar, it is not clear whether Melchizedek is like the Son in every respect or just a perpetual priest. We know that Jesus had a father, a mother, a genealogy, a birth and a death, so He was different in this respect. Scripture does not say that Melchizedek was the Son of God; just that he was 'like' the Son. Melchizedek had no parents that are mentioned in Scripture. Unlike the Levitical priests, his position as priest did not depend on his parents or his genealogy. His priesthood was a different kind, a different order. Scripture says nothing about his birth or death, unlike the patriarchs who are carefully chronicled. He did not create a dynasty of priests, each dying and passing the priesthood to a son.

Jesus was not a Levite, but belonged to the tribe of Judah and no one from that tribe was ever a priest. Moses did not authorize anyone from Judah to be a priest. Jesus was appointed a priest, not by a law that focused on genealogy, but because He lives forever at God's right hand.

From this fact alone, we can see that the Law of Moses is no longer in force. For the law made nothing perfect, but introduced hope by which we draw near to God. Some will ask if Father Abraham and his men paid tithes, who are we not to do so? Brethren, at the time Abraham paid tithes, Christ and His ministry of grace had not been introduced into the scene. Abraham operated in the era of the Old and could not have acted as one in the New. Likewise, we that are in the New ought to act in the New not the Old.

Take special note of the verse that says, "Men that die receive tithes." (Hebrews 7:8) How is it that we don't get it? The Levites reflect the men because they were under the law and bound to it. The death talked of here is not limited only to the physical, but also the spiritual. We all know that the law was inefficient and unable to give life, thus the reason for why Christ came. 1 john 1-2 tells us;

1 That which was from the beginning, which we have heard which we have seen with our eyes, which we have looked upon and our hands have handled, of the word of life;

2 For the life was manifested, and we have seen it, and bear witness, and shew unto you that eternal life, which was with the father, and was manifested unto us.

Had the law been able to give life, the coming of Christ in the flesh would have been of no use. The Bible tells us expressly that we who are born again, filled with the Holy Spirit, are sons of God together with Christ. We are indeed one with Him. We constitute one spiritual person which He is the Head and we are the Body (Romans 12:5). How foolish for us to pitifully decline this position when we have been granted unmerited privilege and inheritance to be one with God through Christ. It makes no sense to embrace a position of death, with no gain, when Christ suffered intensely in the hands of Judas and his gang to redeem us. We live in Jesus Christ, alleluia, what a glorious privilege!

By collecting tithes, we are indirectly changing the priesthood of Christ when God said His priesthood is forever 1. How could you override such wisdom? Clearly from some strange Spirit I guess, because it is not from the Holy Spirit. The Almighty is not a confused God.

Hebrews 7:24-27 says;

24 But this man, because he continueth ever, hath an unchangeable priesthood.

25 Wherefore he is able also to save them to the uttermost that come unto God by him, seeing he ever liveth to make intercession for them.

26 For such an high priest became us, who is holy, harmless, undefiled, separate from sinners, and made higher than the heavens.

27 Who needeth not daily as those high priests to offer up sacrificefirst for his own sins, and then for the people, for this he did once when he offered up himself

Verse 25 makes mention of two very important words that I would like to examine. They are save and uttermost.

1) **Save:** What is Christ saving us from? He is saving us from the devil's invasion of our health, life, salvation and finance, etc.
2) **Uttermost:** We are told that not only does Christ save us from the invasion of the devil, but He saves us uttermost, i.e. to the fullest.

How is it that we pay 10% of our monthly earnings to compensate for our salvation which has been redeemed freely? This is unbelief, the opposite of faith, which the Bible speaks strongly against. Without faith, it is impossible to please God. Brethren, take this as an example. You have been striving to raise money to build your dream house and all the pleasant things therein. Despite all your efforts, you struggle to raise the money. Just as your hope is declining, someone comes up to you and says, "My son, I have seen you stress all these years to raise money for your project. Time to stop struggling; I will build you a house more beautiful than you can imagine." He does so, and you thank him very much. Then every month, you go to him with ten percent of your monthly income, dancing and giving him part payment for that house he built for you freely. Oh, what have we been doing all these years? It is time to stop, turn over a new page and make things right.

In a dream some years ago, I saw myself in a Catholic Church. Filled with people, the preacher was in front of us, but instead of preaching the Word of God, he was busy selling some things and making money from the people. All of a sudden, serious fighting broke out in the Church, members against each other. One of the members came to me and gave me a severe blow on the face. I sat quietly, but he gave me another hit. I did not retaliate, but asked him why they were fighting. He gave me no reply then suddenly the Holy Spirit came into me and took me to a very high place. I took up my right hand then uttered in a loud voice that everyone should stop fighting and listen to what the Holy Spirit has to say. Then the Spirit spoke through me that they should stop everything and start over. I woke soon after. Initially, I had no understanding of what it meant, but as I grew more in touch with my calling, I began to have a clear understanding of what God was saying through the dream. It is part of the reason why you are reading *The Great Outcry* now. The Holy Spirit is pleading with you to change the ways of the past for it is vain and useless. Stop, turn over a new page and start fresh. Verse 26 informs us that a high priest became us; holy, harmless, undefiled, separate from sinners and made higher than Heaven. Yes, not of our own abilities, but of Christ's will. Alone we could not attain that height or life. Verse 27 tells us that we do not need to offer sacrifices daily like in the law, because the Blood of Jesus has been given up freely for our redemption once and for all. That is final. Brethren, we need not slaughter anymore bulls for that purpose. We need not pay tithes any more for the purpose of redeeming our finance. The sacrifice of Christ on the Cross is total and perfect redemption, and covers everything.

WHAT REALLY IS TITHE?

What is tithe and how did God instruct people to use the tithes they collected? Tithe is one of the laws given to the Israelites by God during the time of Moses. The Israelites were expected to give ten percent of their farm produce and their cattle to the Levites who had no inheritance, as seen in Leviticus 27:30-32

30 And all the tithe of the land, whether of the seed of the land, or of the fruit of the tree, is the Lord's; it isholy unto the Lord.

31 And if a man will at all redeem ought of his tithes, he shall add thereto the fifth part thereof.

32 And concerning the tithe of the herd, or of the flock, evenof whatsoever passeth under the rod, the tenth shall be holy unto the Lord.

God specifically said to Moses that the descendants of Levi will inherit tithes from the children of Israel, because they were set aside to priesthood. They were responsible for the services of the tabernacle of the congregation and they had to bear the iniquity of the people. Hebrews 7:5 writes

5 And verily they that are of the sons of Levi, who receive the office of the priesthood, have a commandment to take tithes of the people according to the law, that is, of their brethren, though they come out of the loins of Abraham.

God granted the descendants the rights to receive tithes, because they were of the Old. Those called into service as preachers and evangelists in the New, are to depend entirely on Christ and upon the Holy Spirit. Any other provision would lead them on the wrong path.

Special chambers in the house of the Lord were set aside for the keeping of offerings, tithes and faithfully dedicated things. Cononiah, a Levite, was appointed to look after these offerings, assisted by his brother, Shimei. Every third year, the tithes and produce were reserved as a festival tithe. This means all people united; the Levite, the stranger, the orphan, the widow and the poor came together for a feast. You would not expect those who teach tithing as an obligation to practice the third year tithe.

Even if we were obliged to collect tithes today, this to me would be the most important part – The orphans and the widows, the poor and helpless benefitting from it, but none of these greedy prosperity preachers ever dare make mention of this. People of God why do you insist on being blind?

WAS MONEY TO BE COLLECTED AS TITHES?

No, not at all, the Levites who collected tithes during the days of Moses did not collect a single dime. In fact, the Bible says in the Book of Deuteronomy 14:24-26

Deuteronomy 14:24-26;

24 And if the way be too long for thee, so that thouart not able to carry it, or if the place be too far from thee, which the Lord thy God shall choose to set his name there, when the Lord thy God hath blessed thee:

25 Then shalt thou turn it into money, and bind up the money in thine hand, and shalt go unto the place which the Lord thy God shall choose:

26 And thou shalt bestow that money for whatsoever thy soul lusteth after, for oxen, or for sheep, or for wine, or forstrong drink, or for whatsoever thy soul desireth; and thou shalt eat there before the Lord thy God, and thou shalt rejoice, thou and thy household.

In fact, by the nation Israel tithing under the Law of Moses, they were to trust God, acknowledging that everything belongs to Him. Today, it is impossible to tithe in the same manner for it was mostly agricultural. The tithes were not gifts, they were taxes. Tithes were given in addition to other numerous offerings which estimated to over 22 percent (not just 10 percent). Under the law, if you were only giving 10 percent, you would be robbing God. One tithe was used to support the Levites who were not allowed to own property like the other tribes of Israel. However, this tithe was not money. The goods the Levites received would provide their living for their work in the tabernacle. They also were to tithe on part of the goods that they received, and were to dedicate to the Lord a tenth to the office of the high priest (Numbers 18:21-28). It was the Levites who were to "bring up the tenth of the tithes to the house of our God, to the chambers of the storehouse." (Nehemiah 10:38).

1 Timothy 1:5-7 says, "Now the purpose of the commandment is charity out of a pure heart, and of a good conscience, and of faith

unfeigned, from which some having swerved have turned aside unto vain jangling, desiring to be teachers of the law, understanding neither what they say nor whereof they affirm." This portion of the Bible is speaking directly to you, bishops, archbishops, reverends, professors and doctors of prosperity. The New Testament teaches grace giving. Tithing was not a free will, cheerful giving; it was a commandment in Moses' law to Israel, a nation under God. Nowhere in the New Testament does it require any obligation or a legal portion of one's income.

1 John 2:10-15

10 He that loveth his brother abideth in the light, and there is none occasion of stumbling in him.

11 But he that hateth his brother is in darkness, and walketh in darkness, and knowethnot whither he goeth, becausethat darkness hath blinded his eyes.

12 I write unto you, little children because your sins are forgiven you for his name's sake.

13 I write unto you fathers, because ye have known him that is from the beginning. I write unto you young men, because ye have overcome the wicked one. I write unto you, little children because ye have known the father.

14 I have written unto you, fathers, because ye have known him that is from the beginning. I have written unto you, young men because ye are strong, and the word of God abidethin you, and ye have overcome the wicked one.

14 Love not the world, neither the things that are in the world. If any man loves the world, the love of the father is not in him.

The way prosperity teachers manipulate God's people is more than most scams would dare to do, and they do it with no shame and remorse. They have succeeded to make this awful doctrine a normal and acceptable pattern to be followed by God's children who have turn their backs on the true wisdom and power of God, saying it is God's prescription for His people so they by it can be liberated from the powers of the devil, and if you don't abide by it, they label you out as the abnormal one, and make all the other members in their church who don't see, see you as a potential enemy to be feared and avoided, blinding the ear and eyes of their hearts even more that they may be forever their slaves. What hurts more is the fact that they do it in the name of God. I'm not trying to compel any man to see the way I see, or reason the way I reason, but I'm simply calling on every Christian with very new bibles to pick up the bible, dust it up and try and make it very old. Sit in your closet alone, think, think, think, and think it all up over and over again. What do you think Mathew 7:7 mean? That ask, seek and knock and the doors of money will be opened to you as your prosperity thief tells you brother! Oh no that is not true dear brother, what the Master was saying here is that seek, ask for true wisdom buried up in the word of God, who dwells also in your inside, and the door leading therein will be opened up to you. Have you ever asked yourself why your man of prosperity won't tell you this truth? Come on brother he won't he is defending a venture, and won't be the one to ruin his own business. He will tell you rather to pay for, buy what he is trying to sell to you, brother but have you ever asked yourself this question, someone is asking you to buy some items from someone, where as the person you are to buy from you have Him in you, bodily, and of course all that He possess He has made available to you already, it is in you, you have in you already all that needs to be done is to call it forth and wait, for it to be able to be seen with optical eyes oh brother.

The Apostles made it clear, "But have renounced the hidden things of dishonesty, not walking in craftiness, nor handling the word of God deceitfully; but by manifestation of the truth commending ourselves to every man's conscience in the sight of God." (2 Corinthians 4:2).

Genesis 8:2 teaches us that the windows of Heaven were shut and the rain from Heaven was restrained. Water is consistently used in the Bible. In Genesis, it was a judgment. In Malachi 3, it was a blessing on their crops. The nation lived by their agriculture (Husbandry) and depended on the rain. God's blessing had to do with His provision of water; no rain and they would starve. If they did not give God their tithes, which was part of the blessing in the Mosaic covenant, God would bring a curse upon them; the ground would not yield food because He would not allow it to rain.

Many quote the Book of Malachi as proof that we are to tithe. God is not rebuking the people, but He is rebuking the Levites for keeping the tithe that went to them. Modern day prosperity teachers who use this verse to keep people faithful to them, are either ignorant of its true biblical meaning, or have buried the truth in the oceans of their greed. They like to point out that Jesus commanded tithing. Tithe and tithing are found eight times in the New Testament (Matthew 23:23, Luke 11:42 and 18:12, Hebrews 7:5-6 and 8-9). All of these passages refer to the Old Testament usage under the law. Tithing was still practiced under the law when Jesus was on earth, but the only time Jesus mentioned tithe was when He rebuked religious leaders. "But woe to you Pharisees! For you tithe mint and rue and all manner of herbs, and pass by justice and the love of God. These you ought to have done, without leaving the others undone." In Matthew 23:23, He explains they "have neglected the weightier matters of the law, judgment, mercy and faith." Here, Jesus makes it clear that living the life of faith towards God includes love for man, even more necessary than what you give to God; this was under the law not grace. Think about what Jesus was addressing – Justice. The Pharisees were unfair in their dealings with the people; they took more than their share from the sacrifices brought to the temple. Mercy, they had none, everyone had to be as religious as them, and they looked down upon people.

Let us recall the story Jesus told of the two men who went up to the temple to pray, one a Pharisee and the other a tax collector. The Pharisee stood and prayed to himself, "God, I thank you that I am not like other men, extortioners, unjust, adulterers or even like this tax collector. I fast twice a week and I give tithes of all that I possess." The tax collector, standing in the distance would not so much as raise his eyes to Heaven, but beat his breast, saying, "God, be merciful to me a sinner!" Jesus said, "I tell you, this man went down to his house justified rather than the other; for everyone who exalts himself will be humbled, and he who humbles himself will be exalted." (Luke 18:10-14). So you see, giving is not enough to make one justified before God, yet many have been convinced to rely on their obedience in this area to gain God's blessings.

The Pharisees said they have faith, but they were more interested in the money. Jesus said, "Now the Pharisees, who were lovers of money, also heard all these things, and they derided Him." Nowhere does Paul or any other Apostle in the New Testament mention an obligatory amount. On the other hand, Israel was under the law, being a theocratic nation they were obligated to tithe. Jesus had kept the law before He was crucified, for this reason Jesus had Peter pay the temple tax. After Jesus was crucified, the New Covenant began and the Old was finished. New Testament Christians were never under the Old Covenant law, so one cannot conclude tithing is required under the New Covenant. Not once does any epistle contain any admonitions or a rebuke for failing to tithe. The necessity of giving is mentioned but only with the right attitude, to help and support others. You do not need to tithe to gain God's blessings.

Today, we find the poor desiring to be rich whilst the rich look upon themselves as being blessed and use their abundance as proof of their spiritual condition. They have trained themselves in covetousness ignoring Mark 4:19 says;

19 And the cares of this world, the deceitfulness or riches, and the desires of other things entering in choke the word and it becomes unfruitful.

One can have an abundance of material blessings and still be bankrupt in their spirituality. We have Jesus saying this about the Church of Laodicea. We have too many examples of spiritual giants who have followed the path of abundance to their own demise, Solomon for one. Jesus spoke about money, but often with warnings and rebukes, not as a blessing promised for all who follow Him. From today's prosperity preaching, one would never know Jesus said, "Take heed and beware of covetousness, for one's life does not consist in the abundance of the things he possesses." (Luke 12:15). We are cautioned through the whole body of Scripture to be careful of coveting and pursuing riches.

Solomon, who made more money than most of us will ever dream of, wrote in Proverbs 28:20-23;

20 A faithful man shall abound with blessings: but he that maketh haste to be rich shall not be innocent.

21 To have respect of persons is not good: for for a piece of bread, that man will transgress.

22 He that hasteth to be rich hath an evil eye, and considereth not that poverty shall come upon him.

23 He that rebuketh a man afterwards shall more favor than he that flattereth with the tongue.

Solomon touched on both sides of this issue, being poor and being rich. A faithful man is one who serves the Lord no matter what he owns. In other words, we are to be content with what we have. We can easily focus our pursuit on the blessings without realizing that we have abandoned a spiritual life and moved into a position of severe chastening. Romans 8:32 says;

32 He that spared not His own son, but delivered him up for us all, how shall he not with him also freely give us all things?

We have already been promised what we need according to the love and provision found in Jesus Christ. Many teachers use Mark 10:30 as a promise that anything we give to the Lord will be multiplied one hundred times back to us. Jesus was not speaking about giving, but leaving everything behind to follow Him. In fact, neither money nor giving is mentioned in association with the hundredfold found in Mark. There is no excuse for teaching this and leading the congregation into collective coveting by their giving. Read the passage carefully!

Some people teach that tithing is the only way to support your local church and determine a person's spirituality. Some have gone as far as to assume that tithing is a requirement of salvation. If one does not give 10%, they are not a true Christian. Some even teach from Malachi 3 that you are cursed. What manipulation! Malachi is not just about tithing, but also about the Law of Moses. If you choose by obligation to submit yourself to even part of the Law of Moses, you are obligated to keep it all. If you owe money on your house, do not fall for the scammers who say the money you have saved for the mortgage will not pay for the house so send it in as a seed to get more money, know such a person is a thief, a church rat, feeding on your carnal nature and making you covet. Be responsible to God before man. Scripture does not teach you to give more than you can afford nor give so God can give you more. There was no mention of the poor becoming rich in the Gospel; Jesus did not promise a hundredfold blessing. We learn in Titus 1:1011, "For there are many unruly, vain talkers and deceivers, specially they of the circumcision: whose mouths must be stopped, who subvert whole houses, teaching things which they ought not, for filthy lucre's sake."

Their motivation is money. What is your motivation? It has been said by Author, Sir Roger L'eStrange, that "He that serves God for money will serve the devil for better wages." What did Jesus teach us? You cannot serve God and mammon at the same time. The Church should instead be helping you willingly. That is what they are here for. It is to be the love of Christ that constrains us, for it is the heart of God to help those in need. We, the Church, should be seeking opportunities to give to those less fortunate not give to those who already have it all. I have heard many stories of rich ministries being supported for years versus people who are hurting, yet no help comes their way. Where is your motivation? Is it found in the law or in your heart? The Lord Jesus will reach out and meet the needs of others through us. Love is the principle that governs the Christian's life, it is active not passive. 1 Corinthians 13:3 teaches us, "Though I bestow all my goods to feed the poor, and though I give my body to be burned, and have not charity, it profiteth me nothing."

Jesus did not teach people to give to his ministry day and night, but to help the less fortunate. "Sell what you have and give alms; provide yourselves money bags which do not grow old, a treasure in the heavens that does not fail." (Luke 12:3334). Zacchaeus understood this and said to the Lord, "Look, Lord, I give half of my goods to the poor; and if I have taken anything from anyone by false accusation, I restore fourfold." And Jesus said to him, "Today salvation has come to this house, because he also is a son of Abraham." (Luke 19:89). TODAY He said, today

SALVATION has come, you didn't even care to checkout the meaning of the word salvation from your dictionary, relying one hundred percent on your preachers, think brothers think, do your own findings to be on the safe side do not just swallow anything anyone tries to slice down your throat without taking a close look at it first. Oh Bro! If you want to be blessed, don't give to get more, give from your heart to others who are needy because it is the right thing to do. We should not be supporting false teachers and those who abuse the Gospel for personal gain. We should be supporting those who are sincere and in need. That is doing the Lord's work. Those who are involved in fulltime ministry are to be supported by the people they serve, and those who do ministry and mission work need to be supported by those who are at home with the goods. A careful review of New Testament giving reveals that our contributions should not only support our local church and ministries, but also meet the basic needs of our fellow Christians.

There is NO example of the early Church 'tithing.' In Acts 4:32-37, there were many wealthy Christians who sold portions of their assets and put the money at the Apostles' feet. Was it for the Apostles? No, but for the Christian community, those in need. The Apostles distributed it. The believers were one in heart and mind. The only time we find a judgment having to do with money is in Acts 5:1-11. Ananias and Sapphira were condemned for lying, because they held back part of the proceeds from the sale of the land that they had promised along with everyone else. This had absolutely nothing to do with tithing as much as it had to do with keeping their word. Let your yes be yes, and no be no. Proverbs 22:16 says, "He who oppresses the poor to increase his riches, And he who gives to the rich, will surely come to poverty." The prosperity teachers increase their wealth by making unbiblical promises to the poor, and those who give their money to the teachers are doing what this Scripture says not to. The poor, the homeless, the fatherless, and the widow have always been the focus of God, yet today, they are neglected. How things have changed.

Notes and Reflections for Readers

WHERE DID NEW TESTAMENT TITHE ORIGINATE?

I n this chapter, I decided to use Dr Russell Earl Kelly's article, *Secular History of Tithing*, which can be found in his book entitled, *Should the Church Teach Tithing*. His insightful analysis is worth a read, and promoting.

The "church" was very far from being a united system for many centuries. Competing centers of Christianity arose in Rome, Ephesus, Antioch of Syria, Jerusalem, Caesarea, and North Africa. After the barbarian invasions of the 4th century began, the Roman Empire moved its capital city to Constantinople, where Constantine protected and assisted the church in Constantinople as the most wealthy and influential church for many years to come.

While most church historians will laugh at the thought, not only was tithing NOT a doctrine, it was very far from being discussed by the early church. The locations of the earliest church councils show that Rome was not dominant. The first council at Nicea in A.D. 326 was necessary to discuss the deity of Christ; the second at Constantinople in A.D. 381 was necessary to discuss the deity and person of the Holy Spirit. This was followed by Chalcedon (451); 2nd Constantinople (553); 3rd Constantinople (681); 2nd Nicea (787); 4th Constantinople (869) and, finally, the 1st Lateran Council in Rome in A.D. 1123.

Beginning around the middle of the third century, the tithe only had the authority of a "suggestion" in Cyprian's small area of influence in North Africa. And Cyprian had no authority over other zones of the divided church. Tithing would not even become a local church law for over five hundred years after Calvary. The introduction of tithing emerged in direct proportion to the disintegration of the doctrine of the priesthood of believers and the emergence of the power of the bishop-priests.

New Testament doctrines concerning the church and giving experienced a drastic change from the end of the first apostolic century to the middle of the third century. The *first stage* of decline was the removal of spiritual gifts from the laity. The *second stage* was the distinction of the bishop as a level higher than the other (formerly equal) elders in the church. The *third stage* of decline occurred when the bishop was given a high priestly status with spiritual power over the laity. In the *fourth stage*, the bishops, elders, and (sometimes) the deacons were encouraged to stop performing secular work and devote themselves full-time to the church. Tithing became the *fifth stage* of this doctrinal decline.

Instead of the priesthood of every believer replacing the Old Testament priesthood, the church had gradually reorganized itself to resemble the Old Testament hierarchy. The bishop had become the equivalent to the Old Testament high priest, the presbyters to the Old Testament priests, and the deacons to Old Testament Levites. Full sustenance followed by using the Old Testament pattern of priesthood, sacrifices, and forgiveness controlled by priests. Thus some types of tithing was introduced into the church only after a long period of at least 200-300 years of steady doctrinal decline and only to follow the pattern of Old Testament worship. Even then, tithing was not mandatory or compulsory for many more centuries.

NON-CHRISTIAN JEWS

A noted authority on Judaism, Alfred Edersheim, gives several important points which prove that tithing did not exist in the early centuries of the church. He reminds us of the Jewish customs which were surely followed by at least the Jewish-Christian apostles and disciples. **First,** tithing was not universal, even in Israel, because it did **not** apply

The Great Outcry for the True Gospel This Era

to crafts and trades, "And it is remarkable, that the law seems to regard Israel as intended to be only an agricultural people – no contribution being provided for from trade or merchandise." **Second,** proper tithes could only come from the holy lands of Israel (p. 15-17). **Third,** most Jews considered it a sin to make a profit from teaching the law, "Then, as for the occupation of ordinary life, it was indeed quite true that every Jew was bound to learn some trade or business. But this was not to divert him from study; quite the contrary. *It was regarded as a profanation – or at least declared such – to make use of one's learning for secular purposes, whether of gain or of honor.* The great Hillel had it (Ab. I. 13); 'He who serves himself by the crown [the Torah] shall fade away' (p. 118). **Fourth,** rabbis, such as Paul, were not expected to earn a living from teaching the law, "For, in point of fact, with few exceptions, all the leading Rabbinical authorities were working at some trade, till at last it became quite an affectation to engage in hard bodily labor..." (p. 173). And, **fifth,** honest labor was considered a cherished virtue, "And this same love of honest labor, the same spirit of manly independence, the same *horror of trafficking with the law,* and using it either as a 'crown or as a spade,' was certainly characteristic of the best Rabbis." (p. 172). Edersheim leaves no room in his conclusions for an idea that rabbis might have taught God's law to provide for their own financial sustenance. This very strong tradition among Jews certainly would have been extended into the Jewish Christian Church by former Jewish rabbis, such as Paul.

Later, after the Jews had been banished from the land of Israel, Jewish law was modified concerning tithing. To the question, "How much must a man contribute to charity?" The answer given in the **Code of Jewish Law** involved "tithes," which had become little more than alms. The first year required a tithe of his capital; afterwards he was to tithe net profits. He could choose, instead, to give a fifth of his capital each year, but never more than a fifth. "*The tithe money (set aside for charity) must not be used for the purpose of any other religious act, like buying candles for the synagogue; but it must be given to the poor.*" However, there were exceptions to this rule. Tithes could be used to pay for circumcision, dowry for poor couples wishing to get married, and setting those couples up in a secure trade (p. 1-112). The Jewish sage was expected to either know a craft or learn a craft in order to avoid idleness. In the event that worker did not know or have a craft, the community was to provide a craft or training and help that person as much as possible to earn a living through a trade (p. 1-114). Also, the poorest were still not required to tithe, or give to charity. "But he who has barely sufficient for his own needs, is not obligated to give charity, for his own sustenance takes precedence over another's" (p. 1-111).

JEWISH CHRISTIANS (ESPECIALLY AROUND JERUSALEM)

Almost every denomination's historians of early church history agree that, until A.D. 70 the Jewish Christians in Jerusalem faithfully attended the temple in obedience to Jewish law and, as faithful Jews, supported the Jewish temple with tithes and offerings in addition to their church support. Acts 21:21-24 can hardly lead to any other conclusion!

The Jewish Christians had merely added their unique brand of Judaism into the already diverse Judaism of their day. Although the Sadducees did not accept them, the Pharisees did not oppose them and applauded their high moral conduct within Judaism. Jewish Christians narrowly escaped when the temple was destroyed in A.D. 70 by fleeing to Pella. The final banishment of Jews under Emperor Hadrian in A.D. 132-135 ended all hope of Jewish Christian leadership from Jerusalem. (However, the Gentile Christians had an influential church there in the new Roman city).

From the destruction of Jerusalem until the end of the fourth century the "Nazarenes" were identified with a small group of Jewish Christians who held themselves bound by the Law of Moses, but did not refuse fellowship with Gentile Christians. While later splitting into Pharisaic Ebionites, Essene Ebionites, and Elkaisites, they also considered Paul a false teacher and eventually found themselves outside of the recognized church. *These Jewish Christians never ceased teaching that strict obedience to the Mosaic Law was necessary for salvation.* Thus, for many Jewish Christians, tithing *never* left the spiritual environment of the Mosaic Law.

THE SECOND AND THIRD CENTURY APOSTOLIC AGE UNIVERSAL CHURCH

It is very easy to demonstrate from Scripture that none of the first century post-Calvary Apostolic fathers like Paul, Peter, John, James, Jude and Luke, taught tithing. Several chapters in this book demonstrate that no teaching of tithing exists in Scripture after Calvary.

The second and third generation church leaders (c. A.D. 100-200) were almost totally devoted to living an ascetic (self-denying), or semi-ascetic, lifestyle, preaching the gospel, defending the gospel, and helping the poor and needy. Research this for yourself! They abstained from worldly pleasures and took great pride in doing so. Constructing fine houses of worship and accumulating financial independence were completely foreign to their lifestyle. They took literally Jesus' words in Matthew 19:21, "If you want to be perfect, go, sell that which you have, and give to the poor, and you shall have treasure in heaven; and come, follow me," and Paul's words to elders in Acts 20:35, "I have shown you all things, how that so laboring you ought to support the weak, and to remember the words of the Lord Jesus, how he said, 'It is more blessed to give than to receive.'"

The first generation church fathers wrote very often about the Lord's Supper being the occasion for offerings for the needy. Almsgiving was considered better than both fasting and prayer. *Tithing, however, was not included!* The verifiable *presence* of freewill-giving in their writings, along with the verifiable *absence* of tithing in their writings presents a real dilemma for those who support tithing and insist that it was a valid doctrine of the church from the very beginning. Obtain a copy of the ten-volume **Ante-Nicean Fathers** and settle this issue! Tithe-teachers do not quote the very earliest church leaders in order to validate their doctrinal position.

Robert Baker (Southern Baptist) wrote, "*The leaders [before A.D. 100] usually worked with their hands for their material needs.* There was no artificial distinction between clergy and laity." He later added, "*The earliest bishops or presbyters engaged in secular labor to make their living and performed the duties of their church office when not at work.*"

Alfred Edersheim (Anglican), in his book, *Sketches of Jewish Social Life*, devoted an entire chapter to the Jewish work ethic. "Thus… to come to the subject of this chapter… We now understand how so many of the disciples and followers of the Lord gained their living by some craft; how in the same spirit the Master Himself condescended to the trade of his adoptive father; and how the greatest of his apostles throughout earned his bread through the labor of his hands, probably following, like the Lord Jesus, the trade of his father. For it was a *principle*, frequently expressed, if possible 'not to forsake the trade of the father.'"

Lars P. Qualben (Lutheran) explains this in detail in *A History of the Christian Church*. "The local church had elders and deacons who supervised and directed the work of the congregation, administered its charity, took care of the sick, and saw to it that services were regularly held. But the early church organization was not centered in office and in law, but in the special gifts of the Spirit. The teaching, the preaching, and the administration of the sacraments were conducted by the 'gifted men' in the congregation. An elder might also teach, preach, and administer the sacraments, but he did not do so because he was an elder, but because he was known to have the 'gift.' *None of these 'gifted men' held church office in a legal or judicial sense.* The preaching, the teaching, and the administration of the sacraments were not legally confined to any specific office. The gospel could be preached and the sacraments could be administered in the presence of any assembly of believers, gathered in the name of the Lord."

"Toward the end of the first century a change took place. A general lack of confidence in the special gifts of the Spirit, a desire for more specific order, and a pressing demand for proper safeguard against heresy resulted in a gradual transfer of the preaching, the teaching, and the administration of the sacraments from the 'gifted men' to the local elders…"

"During the second and third centuries another important change took place. Instead of government by a group of elders, the local churches were headed by single officials for whom the name 'bishop' was exclusively reserved… The election of the bishop became a *legal* ordinance and the bishop alone had a right to preach, to teach, and to administer the sacraments…"

Philip Schaff comments on church growth before the great persecutions which followed, "Until about the close of the second century the Christians held their worship mostly in private homes, or in desert places, at the graves of martyrs, and in the crypts of the catacombs. This arose from their poverty, their oppressed and outlawed condition, their love of silence and solitude, and their aversion to all heathen art." (p. 198). "The first traces of special houses of worship occur in Tertullian, who speaks of going to church, and in his contemporary, Clement of Alexandria, who mentions the double meaning of the word *ekkleesia*. About the year 230, Alexander Severus granted the Christians the right to a place in Rome… After the middle of the third century the building of churches began in great earnest…" (pp. 199-200).

"Thus we find, so early as *the third century*, the foundations of a complete hierarchy; though a hierarchy of only moral power, and holding no sort of outward control over the conscience… *With the exaltation of the clergy [in the third century] appeared the tendency to separate them from secular business, and even from social relations… They drew their support from the church treasury, which was supplied by voluntary contributions and weekly collections on the Lord's Day. After the third century they were forbidden to engage in any secular business or even to accept any trusteeship*" (as per Cyprian in North Africa only, p. 128).

While there were many pre-Nicean (pre A.D. 325) early church fathers whose writings still exist, until Cyprian, they did not write about any form of suggested enforced tithing at all. These include Clement of Rome, Mathetes, Polycarp, Ignatius, Barnabas, Papias, Justin, the Pastor of Hermas, Tatian, Theophilus of Antioch, Athenagoras, Clement of Alexandria, Tertullian, Minucius Felix, Commodianus, Origen, Hippolytus, Caius, and Novatium.

In an effort to support early tithing, the **McClintock and Strong Encyclopedia of Biblical, Theological, and Ecclesiastical Literature** actually verifies my claims. Under *tithes* it says, "The obligation from ecclesiastical literature has been put forward from **the earliest period**. The Apostolic Canons [c. 300], the Apostolic Constitutions [c. 300],

St. Cyprian (d. 258], and the works of Ambrose [d. 397], Chrysostom [d. 407], Augustine [d. 430] and the other fathers of both divisions of the Church [East and West, but not Greek] **abound** with illusions to it." For this resource, although "abound" is an exaggeration, "the earliest period" skipped the first 200 years after Calvary. (See Cyprian following).

Clement of Rome (c. 95) began writing about the same time the Apostle John died. His writings do not use the word, "tithe." He is not specific when he wrote, "He [God] has enjoined offerings [to be presented] and service to be performed [to Him], and that not thoughtlessly or irregularly, but at the appointed times and hours" (*First Letter to the Corinthians*, chapter 40). Most likely, at this time, Jewish Christians in the Roman church would have objected to any hint that tithes be taken away from Levitical priests.

Justin Martyr (c. 150) (from the area of old Samaria) wrote, "And *the wealthy among us help the needy...* When our prayer is ended, bread and wine and water are brought, and the president in like manner offers prayers and thanksgiving, *according to his ability*, and the people assent, saying Amen; and there is a distribution to each, and a participation of that over which thanks have been given, and to those who are absent a portion is sent by the deacons. And *they who are well to do, and willing, give what each thinks fit*; and what is collected is deposited with the president, who succors the orphans and widows and those who, through sickness or any other cause, are in want, and those who are in bonds and the strangers sojourning among us" (*First Apology*, chap. 67). In accordance with the first century Scripture, "presidents," or church leaders, are only capable administrators, and not necessarily pastors or teachers of the Word.

Justin's writings only use the word, "tithe," four times: Twice from Matthew 23:23 to point out that the Jews did not like Christ, and twice from Genesis 14:20 while proving that Melchizedek did not require circumcision (*Dialogue with Trypho*, chap. 17, 19, 33, 112).

The ***Didache***, or ***Teaching of the Twelve*** (150-200?), was discovered in the late 19th century at the Jewish Monastery of the Most Holy Sepulcher at Constantinople. It is not known if it is authentic, represents

82

the norm, or is from an aberrant offshoot. It appears to be a Jewish-Christian document from approximately the middle of the second century, and it gives some interesting ideas about how prophets and church leaders were supported.

Paragraph XI... "Now, as concerning the apostles and prophets according to the teaching of the gospel, so do; and let every apostle that comes to you be received as the Lord; and he shall stay but one day, and, if need be, the next day also; but if he stays three days he is a false prophet. When the apostle goes forth, let him take nothing but bread, until he reaches his lodging: *If he asks for money, he is a false prophet...* But whosoever shall say in spirit, 'Give me money, or other things,' you shall not listen to him; but if he bids you to give for others that are in need, let no man judge him."

Paragraph XII may (or may not) only refer to ordinary travelers. Its location between paragraphs 11 and 13 should be considered. "Let every one that 'comes in the name of the Lord' be received" and proven... "If he wishes to abide with you, being a craftsman, let him work and eat. If he has no craft, use your common sense to provide that he lives with you as a Christian, *without idleness*. If he is unwilling to do so, he is a 'Christ monger.' Beware of such."

Paragraph XIII: "But every true prophet that desires to abide with you is 'worthy of his food.' In like manner a true teacher is also, like the laborer, 'worthy of his food.' Therefore you shall take and give to the prophets every **firstfruits** of the produce of the wine-press and the threshing floor, of oxen and sheep. For the prophets are your high priests. *If you have no prophet, give them to the poor...*"

Paragraph XV: "Elect therefore of yourselves bishops and deacons worthy of the Lord, men that are gentle but **not covetous**, true men and approved; for they also minister to you the ministry of the prophets and leaders."

Although many tithe-teachers quote paragraphs XIII and XV to prove that the early church taught tithing and conveniently ignore paragraphs XI and XII, they greatly deceive when they do this! Paragraphs XI and XII make it clear that paragraphs XIII and XV cannot possibly be stretched to teach tithing. The word, tithing, does not even appear.

Also, when the church finally did try to teach tithing, it did not give the whole tithe to the deacons as Paragraph XV would require if they were the Levites. Perhaps this non-authoritative document is placed in the middle of the second century because of some elevation of bishops, but before the authority urged on them by Cyprian. Noticeably, though, the firstfruits match the description of only food items from Numbers 18 and are not the same thing as tithes. Also, it seems that even these would not be totally supported by the church if it were small, but would be required to retain a trade. It is interesting to note that paragraph XIII says, if there is no prophet in the church, then give the firstfruits to the poor.

Irenaeus (150-200) (bishop of Lyons in France and teacher of Hippolytus), clearly did not teach tithing. "And for this reason did the Lord, instead of that [commandment], 'You shall not commit adultery,' forbid even concupiscence; and instead of that which runs thus, 'You shall not kill,' He prohibited anger; and <u>*instead of the law enjoining the giving of tithes, to share all our possessions with the poor*</u>; and not to love our neighbors only, but even our enemies; and not merely to be liberal givers and bestowers, but even that we should present a gratuitous gift to those who take away our goods" (*Against Heresies*, book 4, chap. 13, para. 3). If anything, this teaches extreme asceticism.

"For with Him there is nothing purposeless, nor without signification, nor without design. And for this reason they (the Jews) had indeed the *tithes* of their goods consecrated to Him, *but those who have received liberty set aside all their possessions for the Lord's purposes*, bestowing joyfully and freely not the less valuable portions of their property, since they have the hope of better things [hereafter]; as that poor widow acted who cast all her living into the treasury of God" (*Against Heresies*, book 4, chap. 18). Again, poverty and asceticism are indicated. Irenaeus clearly taught that the church was a dispenser of necessities for the poor. His life and writings reveal that he believed that its leaders should live as meagerly as possible.

Tertullian (150-220) was a prolific writer from Carthage in northern Africa whose writings do not teach tithing. He was also a Montanist who lived an extremely ascetic lifestyle. For the Montanists, extreme poverty was a virtue which allowed absolutely no room for a doctrine of tithing. Since he taught that all incoming offerings should be given to the poor, Tertullian would not have taught that church leaders should be supported through tithes. His only recorded uses of the word, "tithe," appear when he quotes Matthew 23:23 to compare Marcion's hypocrisy with that of the Pharisees (*Marcion*, book 4, chap. 27) and Genesis 14:20 when he argued, like Justin Martyr, that Melchizedek was not circumcised (book 5, chap. 9).

Tertullian also wrote, "Our presidents are elders of proved worth, men who have attained this honor not for a price, but by character. *Every man brings some modest coin once a month or whenever he wishes, and only if he is willing and able; it is a freewill offering.* You might call them the trust-funds of piety; they are spent... On the support and burial of the poor..." (*Apology*, xxxix, 1-18). From these it is clear that, at least near the end of the second century, no tithing existed solely to support full-time clergy.

Cyprian (200-258) followed Tertullian in Carthage (North Africa only) and was probably the first influential leader to suggest (unsuccessfully) that tithes should support a full-time clergy. It must be remembered that, by Cyprian's time at least the first departures from the apostolic age doctrine had occurred. Spiritual gifts had mostly been taken from the laity and placed within various levels of the clergy. The office of bishop had been distinguished above that of elder and presbyter, and each bishop had spiritual power over the laity through the crude sacramental system. Also his church now erroneously compared the bishop to the Old Testament high priest, the presbyters to the Old Testament priests, and the deacons to Old Testament Levites. Cyprian merely took what he thought was the next logical step (in this scenario of the role of bishops) and insisted that the clergy should cease all secular work and depend on tithes for full-time support. At least in the Western church, the Old Testament pattern of priesthood, sacrifices, and forgiveness was now controlled by so-called Christian high priests, Christian priests, and Christian Levites. Such is the context of Cyprian's tithing appeals! Yet all of the pro-tithing apologists I have read point to Cyprian as their prime evidence of early tithing. While only a bishop in Africa, Cyprian did not have authority beyond his own sphere of influence. Those who quote Cyprian to support early church tithing should place their quotation in this limited historical context!

However, Cyprian's tithing still does not qualify as "proof" that the early church taught tithing. Although not as ascetic as the Montanists and his favorite teacher, Tertullian, Cyprian was, nevertheless, an ascetic who gave up his considerable fortune at his baptism. While he strongly advocated that bishops, presbyters, *and deacons* should receive tithes and devote full-time service to the church, he did not suggest that they should live above the poverty level (*Letter* 65, para. 1). At one occasion, in his *Letter 4*, he said that the "whole of the small sum which was collected" was given to the clergy *and they distributed it to those in need.* Any person who has read Cyprian knows of his generation's many uses of Christ's injunction, "If you want to be perfect, go and sell that you have, and give to the poor, and you shall have treasure in heaven, and come and follow me." Cyprian's understanding of tithing was that church leaders should only take the *bare minimum* and distribute the remainder to the poor. Read Cyprian yourself!

The Constitutions of the Holy Apostles (book 2, section 4), is a fictional account probably dating from the third or fourth century. It was not accepted by the Church until many centuries later. Its use of tithing reflects an evolution of the doctrine to about the same level as that of Cyprian.

"On the Management of the Resources Collected for the Support of the Clergy and the Relief of the Poor:"

"Let the bishop esteem such food and raiment sufficient as suits necessity and decency. Let him not make use of the Lord's goods as another's, but moderately; 'for the laborer is worthy of his reward.' Let him not be luxurious in diet, or fond of idle furniture, but contented with so much alone as is necessary for his sustenance."

"On Firstfruits and Tithes, and After What Manner the Bishop is Himself to Partake of Them, or Distribute Them to Others"

XXV. Let him use those *tenths and first-fruits*, which are given according to the command of God, as a man of God; as also let him dispense in a right manner the free-will offerings which are brought in on account of the poor, to the orphans, the widows, the afflicted, and strangers in distress, as having that God for the examiner of his accounts who has committed the disposition to him. Distribute to all those in want with righteousness, and yourselves use the things which belong to the Lord, but do not abuse them, eating of them, but *not eating them all up by yourselves*: Communicate with those who are in want, and thereby show yourselves unblameable before God. For if you shall consume them by yourselves, you will be reproached by God...."

"For those who attend upon the Church ought to be maintained by the Church, *as being priests, Levites, presidents, and ministers of God; as it is written in the book of Numbers concerning the priests...*"

"Those which *were then* first-fruits, and *tithes*, and offerings, and gifts, *now* are oblations, which are presented by holy bishops to the Lord God, through Jesus Christ, who has died for them. For these are your high priests, as the presbyters are your priests, and your present deacons instead of your Levites; as are also your readers, your singers, your porters, your deaconesses, your widows, your virgins, and your orphans: But He who is above all these is the High Priest."

XXVI. "*The bishop*, he is the minister of the word, the keeper of knowledge, the *mediator* between God and you in the several parts of your divine worship. He is the teacher of piety; and, *next after God, he is your father*, who has begotten you again to the adoption of sons by water and the Spirit. He is your ruler and governor; *he is your king* and potentate; he is, next after God, *your earthly God*, who has a right to be honored by you."

XXVII. "You ought therefore, brothers, to bring your sacrifices and your oblations to the bishop, as to your high priest, either by yourselves or by the deacons; and do you bring not those only, but also your first-fruits, and your *tithes*, and your free-will offerings to him. For he knows who they are that are in affliction, and gives to every one as is convenient, that so one may not receive alms twice or more often the same day, or the same week, while another has nothing at all."

[My comments on the *Constitutions of the Apostles*. While attempting to use the language of the Old Testament Law, several differences are apparent. First, now the high priest, not the Levites, receives the tithes directly. Second, the bishop is to maintain a bare sustenance level from what he takes from the tithes and offerings. Third, the bishop is directly responsible for re-distributing both tithes and offerings back to the needy. Fourth, the new priestly caste system does not refer to Abraham's tithe to Melchizedek in Genesis 14 for pre-Law justification, nor to "It is holy to the Lord" in Leviticus 27:30 for an eternal principle. Clearly, the justification for re-introducing tithing into this particular early church, even if only a voluntary offering, was the result of the abandonment of the doctrine of the priesthood of the believer and the elevation of the position of priest and high priest. Therefore, it is easy to understand why modern Protestant tithe-teachers do not appeal to this document for validation of tithing as a legitimate doctrine. Finally, even this document was rejected by the Roman Catholic Church because tithing did not become church Law until the end of the sixth century.]

THE CHURCH FROM THE FOURTH CENTURY UNTIL THE EIGHTH CENTURY

The church in the first centuries had a very different use for money than the typical church today. Williston Walker reports that, in the year A.D. 251, the Church of Rome under Bishop Grainelius had a membership of approximately 30,000 members and supported over 1,500 dependents. This amounts to one dependent per 20 members!

Although Cyprian tried to enforce his idea that church workers should not pursue secular trades, Walker comments, "By the middle of the third century the higher clergy were expected to give their whole time to the work of the ministry, *yet even bishops sometimes shared in secular business, not always of a commendable character. The lower clergy could still engage in trade.*"

It may, or may not, be noteworthy that Schaff does not mention church "buildings" until the lapse of persecution between 260-303. It is unclear to what extent church edifices existed prior to this time. As long as Christians were blamed for almost every disaster such as famines, earthquakes, floods, battle losses, and barbarian invasions, the pagan population very often punished the church as its scapegoat and would have quickly destroyed highly visible and accessible structures associated with the church.

The ***Encyclopedia Americana*** says, "It [tithing] was *not* practiced in the early Christian church, but gradually became common by the 6th century." The statement assumes Cyprian's failure in North Africa and probably means that tithing was not practiced "by enforcement of Church or secular law" until the 6th century.

The ***Catholic Encyclopedia*** **(1912 edition only)** says, "In the beginning [provision] was supplied by the spontaneous support of the faithful. In the course of time, however, as the Church expanded and various institutions arose, it became necessary to make laws which would insure the proper and permanent support of the clergy. The payment of tithes was adopted from the Old Law, and early writers speak of it as a divine ordinance and an obligation of the conscience. The earliest positive legislation on the subject seems to be contained in the letter of the bishops assembled at **Tours in 567** and the **Canons of the Council of Macon in 585.**"

While it may appear that both the *Encyclopedia Americana* and the *Catholic Encyclopedia* ignore all of the tithing references made by Cyprian and the *Constitutions of the Apostles* as invalid, actually, they must be agreeing with the premise of this book that the early church did not teach tithing! When tithing was first re-introduced into the church, it was voluntary and was built on an erroneous comparison of the New Covenant bishop as a high priest to the Old Testament priesthood.

Centuries later, the church acquired wealth in the form of land. At first wealthy landowners donated land to the church for parishes, but retained the privileges of nominating the bishops and keeping the profits and tithes from the land in their own secular hands. Therefore, tithing soon became a source of abuse. Eventually, however, the church gained enough secular authority to regain appointment of its own priests and bishops again, along with keeping the tithes in the church. The church soon owned from one half to one fourth of the land in many European countries and enacted tithes from those who rented its lands.

Historians usually agree that, not until A.D. 567, five hundred and thirty seven (537) years after Calvary, did the Church's *first* substantial attempt to enforce tithing under its own authority appear in history! The Council of Tours in 567 and the Council of Macon in 585 enacted *regional* church decrees for tithing and excommunication of non-tithers, but did not receive authority from the king to enforce collection through civil decrees. It is significant that tithing did not emerge historically until the church became powerful in the secular realm. Even at this late date tithes were still only food. Eventually the Roman Church even refused to administer last rites if it was not given wealth or land in wills.

Between 774 to 777 the Frankish king, Charlemagne, destroyed the Arian Lombard kingdom which separated his empire from northern Italy. After his defeat of the Lombards, Charlemagne's unopposed rule included northern Italy and Rome. By quoting the Mosaic Law as its authority at a Church synod, the pope finally convinced Charlemagne to allow enforced agricultural tithing in support of the fast-growing parish system of churches. In 785 Pope Hadrian attempted to impose tithing on the Anglo-Saxons. In appreciation of his church support, on Christmas Day, A.D. 800, the pope crowned Charlemagne as Holy Roman Emperor, thus making official the renewed "Holy" Roman Empire.

In 906 King Edgar legally enforced food tithing in England. In 1067 and 1078, at the Church Councils of Gerona, and in 1215 at the Fourth Lateran Council, tithing was increasingly applied to all lands under Christian rule. All citizens, including Jews, were required to tithe to the Roman Catholic Church. A typical peasant was giving the first tithe of his land to his secular ruler or landlord (which was often the church) and a second tenth to the church outright. In 1179 the Third Lateran Council decreed that only the pope could release persons from the obligation to tithe, and he exempted the Crusaders.

For several centuries the right to collect agricultural tithes shifted back and forth between the Church and the secular authority – depending on which was the strongest power. Pope Innocent III (1198-1216), in order to strengthen and purify the church, ordered that tithes for the support of the church be given precedence over all other taxes, excluded all lay interference in church affairs, and prohibited any one man from drawing the income from more than one church office. Theologian **Thomas Aquinas** defended tithing by stating, **"During the time of the New Law the authority of the Church has established the payment of tithes"** (*Summa Theologica,* **Vol. 3, The Second Part of the Second Part). He did use Genesis 14 and Melchizedek to substantiate his argument.**

Exacting agricultural tithes from Jews became especially severe in England and Germanic countries. Beginning around the 14th century, Jews were not even allowed to own land in many nations. This forced the Jews off the land and many went into banking and commerce because those occupations and money were not included in tithing. In 1372 even the clergy in Germany revolted at having to pay tithes to the pope.

Not long after the Bible had been translated into the language of the common man, Otto Brumfels in 1524 proclaimed that the New Testament does not teach tithing. Later that century, Pope Gregory VII, in an effort to control secular ownership of tithes, once again outlawed lay ownership of tithes.

In 1714 the English Anglican exacted agricultural tithes from Roman Catholics and Presbyterians for the support of the Church of Ireland. Soon revolt became ripe in France. Some of the earliest stages of the French Revolution were actions which struck at the privileges and status of the Roman Catholic Church.

In 1789, tithes were abolished in France by the secular authority.

Other revolts against tithing followed. Between 1836 and 1850 tithing was mostly abolished in England. It was later commuted to a rental to be paid in cash. In 1868, as a result of agitation which began at least as far back as the 1830s and which was pushed by Dissenters, the compulsory payment of local parish tithes for the maintenance of the church was abolished and was made purely voluntary. However, the final tithe rent charges were not abolished until 1936 in England.

In Canada, as late as 1868, the Fourth Council of Quebec declared that tithing was mandatory. For a while tithes were even made mandatory in the French lands of the New World until the territory was sold in the Louisiana Purchase. In 1871 tithes were abolished in Ireland. In 1887 they ended in Italy. In West Germany residents must formally renounce church membership in order to avoid mandatory church taxation. Elsewhere, the Eastern Orthodox Church has never accepted tithing and its members have never practiced it. The Roman Catholic Church still prescribes tithes in countries where they are sanctioned by law, and some Protestant bodies still consider tithes obligatory.

Today most religious bodies have abandoned the practice of compulsory tithing, particularly in the United States, where no system of tithing was ever generally employed after the American Revolution. Tithing was never a legal requirement in the United States. Nevertheless, members of certain churches, including the Latter Day Saints and Seventh-Day Adventists are required to tithe and some Christians in other churches do so voluntarily. Southern Baptists define tithing as an "expectation" and some of its churches are pushing to make tithing a requirement for membership (in addition to holding church offices). For further study, most books on church history briefly discuss the history of tithing since Bible times. As Europe slowly rejected church-state taxation and the divine right of kings, it also rejected enforced tithing to state-supported churches.

Relevant to this book, the biblical model of tithing best fits a church-state economy similar to Israel's theocracy. History reveals that tithing became a "Christian" doctrine only after the Roman Catholic Church joined hands with secular and political forces. However, just as tithing was an unprofitable ordinance which never produced spiritual growth in national Israel under the Old Covenant, even so tithing never led to spiritual growth when used by Christians and was eventually forced into retirement a second time by state churches.

Both Roman Catholics and Protestants have been guilty of oppression and persecution regarding state mandated tithing laws. And, like Old Covenant tithing in national Israel, nothing good has ever resulted from such attempts to enforce tithing on another.

Notes and Reflections for Readers

SOWING OF SEEDS

This is another crucial subject that is closely associated with tithing, that the great outcry seeks by the grace of God to redress. Hard is it to believe the extent to which malicious and misguided preachers out there in their numbers, promising their faithful church members financial prosperity and harvest from God as a result of them sowing their money in the house of God have gone, with this illegal doctrine of the old. This has ruined the lives of countless people, led to the death of many, broken up homes and worst of all turned many away from God. All because they have been fooled and robbed of their money they sowed. This in turn, has caused them who still in their ignorance to blame God whom they feel has let down whilst the pastors, doctors and professors of prosperity keep filling their pockets rapidly, saying to their partners hey man, lets make haste in this our mischief before the sheep become lions. They live a flamboyant lifestyle whilst some of their church members cannot even afford daily wholesome meals. Some have to trek for hours back there in Africa, because they have been brainwashed to sow even their last dime which they should be using to pay for transport back home. They are tricked by rebels using the portion of the Bible which mentions the widow who gave more than every other person because she gave all she had.

This extreme heartlessness has left me, and many out there with a heavy burden. By the grace of God and the light of my calling, my eyes have become open to the truth. So much that when I started writing this book, I worked day and night so that I can arrive at this chapter to ease my burden on paper. I make mention here of a man, whom yet his name have I withheld, has sold himself, wholly to greed and the love of money. He I decided to use, after researching on many, of his like as a case study Peter Domingo, is the name I am made compelled to use, a chief perpetrator of evil manipulation and deceit, my apologies for those who believe so very much on him, but I must tickle you up thoroughly to think twice. No wonder when I did some research on his biography, I found a sharp contrast between him and someone like Dwight Moody, a true man of truth, whose heart ached for the lost Souls. We are told in Moody's biography that he was from a poor family and a school dropout. God sowed in his Spirit an incredible desire for the lost, so much that it pained him terribly if a day passed by without him winning over a Soul to God. By contrast, we don't see any drop of love and compassion within Domingo, it is a complete stranger to him. Instead, he is highly credited in his biography for his genius ability to manipulate the minds of the people and extort money. No wonder we are told that Domingo claims to have received the vision for World Changing Ministries Christian Center in 1982, but for what? Darkness or light? We are told he held the Church's first worship service in the cafeteria of Saint Johns M Elementary School in College Park Atlanta. With only eight people in attendance, he successfully received over $100 in contributions. Such a shame brothers and sisters that the desire has turned towards money rather than a burning desire for Souls. Over the years, the ministry has grown rapidly.

As of 2008, the congregation has grown to 31,000 members with $69 million in revenue (gross cash collections for 2006). The congregation moved from its original cafeteria location to a modest-sized chapel, adding a weekly radio broadcast and four services each Sunday. On December 24, 1995, WCCI moved into its present location, the 8,500-seat sanctuary known as the World Dome. At a cost of nearly $18 million, it is claimed that the World Dome was built without any bank financing. What a sad way to credit and rank a man of God who claims to be showing thousands of people the 'right path to salvation.'

In his messages, this man informs people that if it wasn't for the Blood of Jesus, he would take all the non-tithers to one corner of the

Church and shoot them dead then bury them. Disgraceful to hear such words uttered by supposed bearers of Light who in the actual fact are leading the children of God more into utter darkness. Domingo is a fine talker, a legend in the act who knows very well how to get money out of his culprits even against their will. He mimics them sometimes, in a subtle and playful manner, stirring them to bring forth their money while they voice a big Amen! In one of his messages, he quoted 1 Chronicles 29:1-5 saying;

1 Furthermore, David the king said unto all the congregation, Solomon my son, whom alone God hath chosen, is yet young and tender, and the work is great: for the palace is not for man, but for the Lord God.

2 Now I have prepared with all my might for the house of my God the gold for the things to be made of gold, and the silver for the things to be made of silver, and the brass, for the thins of brass, the iron for the things of iron, and wood for the things of wood; onyx stones, and stones to be set, glistering stones and of divers colours, and all manner of precious stones, and marble stones in abundance.

3 Moreover because I have set my affection to the house of my God, I have of mine own proper good, of gold and silver which I have given to the house of my God over and above all that I have prepared for the holy house.

4 Even three thousand talents of gold, of the gold of Ophir, and seven thousand talents of refined silver, to overlay the walls of the houses withal:

5 The gold for the things of gold, and the silver for the things of silver, and for all manner of work to be made by the hands of artificers. And who then is willing to concecrate his service this day unto the Lord?

He speaks nonsense, convincing people to contribute money for his enrichment. He teaches vile doctrines saying harvest responds only to seed not to prayer. In this new era, the burden should be upon those called to bring the gospel of truth (the true seed) to the hearts of the lost, for we know that the temple of God in this new era of grace our body, wherein, in the innermost part of it, (the Hollies of Hollies, ie our spirits). Am I saying we should not support the works of God? No, not at all but in doing so, we should critically consider what great Paul of the New taught. He was a great teacher of the gospel, never took advantage of people's ignorance and did not rob them of their money. His teachings were surrounded by love, honesty and truth.

The Bible says my people are destroyed for lack of knowledge (Hosea 4:6). Brethren, you have allowed these men to destroy you, because you have forsaken the wisdom of God for things of lesser value. It does not make sense to put the cart before the horse; it is time to turn over a new page and start fresh. In his messages, Domingo calls non-tithers and non-seed sowers dishonest and crooks; pathetic titles that describe him best. He goes on further to say that to know a true child of God, you should find out where his treasure is. If he puts his treasure in art, you will find his treasure in art, if he puts his treasure in commodities, you will find his treasure in commodities, and if he puts his treasure in the kingdom of God, you will find his treasure in the kingdom of God. He quoted Matthew 6:21

21 For where your treasure is, there will your heart be also.

He even requests to see their checkbook and calendar, so he could judge where their heart is. Brother, why are you so wicked? How could you afford to be this heartless? To embrace a better understanding of the Book of Matthew which has been twisted by this man, I suggest you read Matthew 6:19-24 Mathew 6:19-24;

19 Lay not up for yourselves treasures upon earth where moth and rust doth corrupt, and where thieves do not break through nor steal:

20 But lay up for yourselves treasures in heaven, where neither moth nor rust doth corrupt, and where thieves do not break though nor steal:

21 For where your treasure is, there will your heart be also.

22 The light of the body is the eye: if therefore thine eye be single, thy whole body shall be full of light.

23 But if thine eye be evil, thy whole body shall be full of darkness. If therefore the light in thee be darkness, how great is the darkness!

24 No man can serve two masters: for either he will hate the one and love the other; or else he will hold to the one, and despise the other. Ye cannot serve God and mammon.

To get a better understanding of the term 'treasure,' below are three definitions:

1) Wealth or riches stored or accumulated, especially in the form of precious metals, money, jewels or plate.
2) Wealth, rich materials or valuable things.
3) Any thing or person greatly valued or highly prized:

We can see that the term 'treasure' does not only refer to riches in money, materials and valuable things, but also to anything greatly valued. From the above three definitions, we can see that the man, Domingo Peter conceals the full meaning of treasure to pinpoint whatever suits him; a master of deceit filling his own pockets. In the third definition, treasure is seen as anything or person greatly valued or highly prized. How is this relevant to Matthew 6:19-29? We are told in verses 19-21, "Not to lay up for yourselves treasures upon earth, where moth and rust doth corrupt, and where thieves break through and steal. But lay up for yourselves treasures in heaven, where neither moth nor rust doth corrupt, and where thieves do not break through nor steal. For where your treasure is, there will your heart be also." What does this mean? Matthew's point is seen in verses 22-23, where he says, "The light of the body is the eye: if therefore thine eye be single, thy whole body shall be full of light. But if thine eye be evil, thy whole body shall be full of darkness. If therefore the light that is in thee be darkness, how great is that darkness!" How? Very simple, he is telling us that our treasure should be that which cannot be destroyed by mold and rust. God gives us the prescription of how to lay hold of this treasure. If we truly want to seek God, we should seek Him for the love of Him. That alone will allow us to see and comprehend things in His light which is love. If we have a double motive of seeking Him, with minds polluted by greed and lust for materialism, then our ability to see will be darkened by the evil of greed. He confirms this in verse 24, "No man can serve two masters: for either he will hate the one, and love the other."

Paul says in his letter to Galatians 1:6-12

6 I marvel that ye are so soon removed from him that called you into the grace of Christ unto another gospel:

7 Which is not another; but there be some that trouble you, and would pervert the gospel of Christ.

8 But though we, or an angel from heaven preach any other gospel, unto you than that which we have preached unto you, let him be accursed.

9 As we said before, so say I now again, if any man preach any other gospel unto you than that ye have received, let him be accursed.

10 For do I now persuade men, or God? Or do I seek to please men? For if I yet pleased men, I should not be the servant of Christ.

11 But I certify you, brethren, that the gospel which was preached of me is not after man.

12 For I neither received it of man, neither was I thought it, but by the revelation of Christ.

I will like you brethren to take very special note of verse 12 and see with me in the eyes of Paul that the true gospel of Christ can not be given by man, but by revelation of Christ, through the spirit.

In one of his YouTube videos, Peter Domingo says that if you want blessings, pay first. It shocks me to hear the people shout a mighty Amen. Where does this man get such babaric ideas from? The Bible says in Romans 8:32,

"He that spared not his own Son, but delivered him up for us all, how shall he not with him also freely give us all things?"

We don't need to give out of fear or pressure, but rather give freely the way we have received freely. The Lord God Almighty has been communicating with some of these men in private to get them to stop what they are doing, but they yield not. Now God is fiercely warning, and calling on them to wake up, and come out of their dead beds. The wise need to repent now and cease such evil acts; the stubborn ones will continue to enjoy the evil gotten wealth whilst expecting the hand of God upon him.

In the book of Titus 1:10-11, Paul tells us that;

For there are many unruly and vain talkers and deceivers, especially they of the circumcision, whose mouths must be stopped, who subvert whole houses, teaching things, which they ought not, for filthy lucre's sake

Some people will ask, "What about the great miracles they are performing? How is that possible without God's Hand upon it? You must remember that not all signs and wonders are from God. You must be on guard and discern, because even the devil is capable of performing wonders that will deceive the children of God. When Moses confronted the pharaoh before delivering the Hebrews from Egypt, he was challenged by the pharaoh's magicians who also performed signs, but their signs weren't from God. Such signs have setbacks and repercussions.

Notes and Reflections for Readers

NOTES AND REFLECTIONS FOR READERS

Seeds in the Old Testament

In the whole of the old testament, there is no record anywhere, of money sowed to the ground, for it to germinate, grow and bear forth fruits for the sower to reap. No where, from Genesis to Malachi, do we have such craziness. Corn and wheat are the seeds mentioned in the old testament. Genesis 26:12 says;

12 Then Isaac sowed in the land, and received in the same year, an hundred fold: and the Lord blessed him.

Isaac sowed his seeds on the land, and not in the temple. He did not till the ground and sow money, for we all know that when someone tills the soil, they sow crops. Truth is, today's preachers promise you freedom, where as they are actually enslaving you, and make your situation even more worse. They have given themselves completely over to the love of money, and this has destroyed their desire to win Souls for God in honesty and sincerity or the desire to help a brother in need. You want to know why? It is simple, Mathew tells us in his gospel Mathew 6:24 that;

24 No one can serve two masters. Either he will hate the one and love the other, or he will be devoted to the one and despise the other, you can't serve both God and mammon.

Mammon can be defined simply as the personification of money, putting it in the place of God. While in Milan, I was attending a Church and the pastor preached a message one Sunday that got me extremely worried. She entitled the message 'Exchanging alter for alter.' She went on to say that most of us pick up our phones and call her from time to time requesting to see her. We come bare handed, yet when we go to see the native doctor, we go with tubers of yams, goats, whisky, you name it.

That we treasure native doctors more than men of God. She said that when she goes to see the senior pastor's wife, she gives her no less than three to five thousand dollars, because she knows what she is going to receive from the woman of God.

How wrong to think that we must give God money, to get what we need from Him, as though we made him a money offer in the first place, to get him to the cross.

Of course, I knew for sure that she was referring to me, because during that period, I was very curious to know more about the Word of God, thus I would call her from time to time, so we could share on some topics in the Bible. I was heartbroken and could not hide it anymore. My countenance changed, there was a lady sitting beside me who believed every word the pastor spoke, as she shouted a very mighty amen, confirming every word that came out of the pastor's mouth. I felt sorry for the young lady, and I opened up Galatians 5:4 for her to read;

4 Christ is become of no effect unto you, whosoever of you are justified by the law; ye are fallen from grace.

All what the pastor is saying are nothing but lies sister, I told the young lady. All she is operating in malice, twisting up the true meaning of the Scripture, to mean something else, to extort money from the people. As I spoke further to the lady, the pastor sensed I was talking against her teachings, thus she told me to stop talking and that we should listen but to her alone. One cannot really expect any better from the pastor, for she has made herself totally dependent upon man. Her mentor, general overseer and founder of the church, encourages the same greedy behavior, collected one thousand naira from each person that came to attend the New Year's Eve service at his Church in Nigeria. He justified it by saying that the levy was for non-regular members who only come on such occasions. Brethren, there can be no justifications under the Heavens for collecting money from people before they can hear the Word of God. We should be happy to see people make an effort to hear the Word of God even if it is only once a year. God has brought them in, and He will touch and renew them from the inside out, at his own time, for them to become consistent and regular members. The Word of God should be given freely like the air we breathe.

After service that day, on my way home, I asked God in my heart how and why He allows such selfish things to happen. My heart was so troubled that when I reached home and slept, God showed me something in a dream. In the dream, I was in that same Church. Someone was crying for help as he was dying, but the pastor and elders were busy counting money, giving a deaf ear to the man's cries. I walked up to them and asked them if they had not heard the dying man cringe for help, but no one noticed me. They continued to count money they had made for that day from tithes, offerings and selling of rhapsody of reality, etc. I got really angry and kicked the table in front of them, ran to the dying person whom God miraculously healed. I started preaching then I immediately woke up from sleep. Brethren, this is the unfortunate message of salvation we get from many Churches today in Europe. I have not been to America, but thank God for YouTube as I can listen to whoever's message in whatever part of the world. It is a heartbreaking catastrophe. Brethren, have we forgotten Acts 8:4-20, which says;

4 Therefore they that were scattered abroad went every where preaching the word.

5 Then Philip went down to the city of Samaria, and preached Christ unto them.

6 And the people with one accord gave heed unto those things which Philip spake, hearing and seeing the miracles which he did.

7 For unclean spirits, crying with loud voice, came out of many that were possessed with them: and many taken with palsies, and that were lame, were healed.

8 And there was great joy in that city.

9 But there was a certain man, called Simon which beforetime in the same city used sorcery, and bewitched the people of Samaria, given out that himself was some great one:

10 To whom they all gave heed, from the least to the greatest, saying, this man is the great power of God

11 And to him they had regard, because that of long time he had bewitched them with sorceries.

12 But when they believed Philip preaching the things concerning the kingdom of God, and the name of Jesus Christ they were baptized, both men and women.

13 Then Simon himself believed also: and when he was baptized he continued with Philip, and wondered, beholding the miracles and signs and wonders which were done.

14 Now when the apostles which were at Jerusalem heard that Samaria had received the word of God, they sent unto them Peter and John:

15 Who, when they were come down, prayed for them, that they might receive the Holy Ghost:

16 (For as yet he was fallen upon none of them: only they were baptized in the name of the Lord Jesus)

17 Then laid they their hands on them, and they received the Holy Ghost.

18 And when Simon saw that through laying on the apostles' hands the Holy Ghost was given, he offered them money,

19 Saying, Give me also this power, that on whomsoever I lay hands, he may receive the Holy Ghost.

20 But Peter said unto him, Thy money perish with thee because thou hast thought that the gift of God may be purchased with money.

Let your money perish with you, if you think the gifts of God can be bought.

Leroy Thompson the one that boasts of his 16,000 dollar dog, a good friend and partner of domingo in one of his videos on YouTube, said whilst preaching, the people brought money to him, but they did not know why they were donating. If I may ask, why would you throw your money to such damnable pimps? Have you nothing to do with your money? Don't you notice hungry men on the streets? Go to Mother Africa, where you come from, there you will find people starving to death. Reaching out to a poor and hungry fellow is directly reaching out to God. You are only paying him for the formidable abominations he is teaching you. If you find such men, you should flee from them, for these men do not have the love of God or the love of the lost in them, but their love is on money. They have sold their souls to the love and lust for money, and have become slaves, to a bigger slave. They are not free men and their words come from their dead hearts. We all know that there can be no life in a dead heart. True life is in love, wherein dwells Christ and truth. Therefore, where there is no love, there is no Christ and therefore no life. The bible says in Luke 12:15;

15 And he said unto them, Take heed, and beware of covetousness: far a man's life consisteth not in the abundance of things which he possesseth.

In the Church which Thompson spoke that nonsense, one could spot out people, God's children, thirsty and hungry for the truth, love and peace of Christ. Young and old, rich and poor, all sorts come to you with hearts yearning for the treatment of the Soul, the true Word of God. Thompson, what have you people been doing to God all these years? I use no title when referring to you guys, because mere man made title is in itself very empty and amounts to nothing, forget about all those big titles you guys ascribe to yourselves, with which you facilitate your task. We really should not respect titles, big names or money, but LOVE which is the beginning and the end of the gospel of Christ (good news).

Here in Belgium, I decided to go visit a friend who lives in Antwerp. I got out of the train station, walked for about 300 meters, crossed the traffic, bent to my right then walked a few more meters. There on my left was a big Church with a visible signboard that read, 'Jesus Christ Is The Lord Help Center.' Standing in front of the sign was a young man distributing fliers. He offered me one, so I stretched forth my hand and collected the flier. It was an invitation, with different people giving testimonies of how their lives have been transformed since they came in contact with the Church. Of all the testimonies, four in total, two in English and two in Dutch, this one gained my attention the most. It is the testimony of one black guy named Isaac. The title of his article, *My financial life has been restored*, read;

"For three years, I had immigration problems and financially life was difficult. I couldn't further my studies let alone work. The worst moment of my life was when I found myself completely penniless. I needed 3000 pounds to apply for my indefinite leave to remain. After much persistent and prayers, I was able to get a percentage of the savings. It was also at that same time that a family member gave me money out of the blue, which in the end, added up to make enough for my application. I was told that the whole process would take almost six months for me to get my response, however after I had made my sacrifice, it only took three weeks and I received my indefinite leave to remain."

No mention of Jesus Christ or salvation by His cross on the flier. Only well calculated and framed up words to motivate the people not to come and be saved, but to come and give money. On one good Sunday, I decided to visit the Church. It was a very big Church, well decorated, very clean with newly painted white walls and a giant screen at the pulpit. The pastor was dressed in a white and purple garment together with his servants. I went and sat on the second to the last seat. Standing beside me was the wife of the pastor; a white lady with long curly black hair. She was dressed in a white garment with shiny eyes that revolved to and fro the ends of the Church. When the sermon started, nothing was said that related to salvation. Nor did I even hear him mention the name of Jesus Christ. All I heard from his mouth was money, money,

money. That we have to serve God with all we have, for He is a God that never fails and is always there standing and ready to pay us back. He who gives to God receives a hundredfold. Soon after he switched on the screen behind him and a man, who claimed to be a man of God, spoke of how he was once very wealthy and decided to put God to the test. He gave his all to support the Church's finance, and in return, God blessed him a hundred times more and therefore he became one hundred times richer. He narrated other bull stories; I don't know where he got them from, but they weren't from God. Any person who does not have a good mastery of the Word of God would be easily deceived by the sweet talks of this one very bad clique. After his partner concluded talking, the preacher encouraged those who are ready to give God their all and put Him to the test to raise their hands. They were collecting cash, cheques and bank transfers. A handful of people went up and I truly felt sorry for them. They seek God not for the love of God, but for greed, hoping they receive great financial returns, but brethren, you should embrace this truth that God is love. He cannot be seen with the optical eyes, neither can he be bought with the substance of our hands, but His powerful and invisible Spirit dwells in love, so those who seek God must go to His dwelling place. Same goes for those who seek a pastor for guidance, they must go to his physical abode. While all these things were happening, I took out my mobile phone and began filming the whole scenario, but the wife walked up to me and forbade me, saying I could not make any video or take pictures without the pastor's authorization. To my additional surprise, she insisted I delete the video I had. In total frustration and grief, I stood up, took my Bible and left. Beware brethren, be wise and vigilant. Let the Word of God be your yardstick to measure up the words that come out of the mouth of anyone claiming to be a servant of God. Not all of them are sincere. Many are uneasily detectable going out in sheep clothes whereas their real identity is wolf skin. The Bible says in 2 Peter 2:1-3

2 Peter 2:1-3

1 But there were false prophets also among the people, even as there shall be false teachers among you, who privily shall bring in damnable

heresies, even denying the lord that bought them, and bring upon themselves swift destruction.

2 And many shall follow their pernicious ways; by reason of whom the way of truth shall be evil spoken of.

3 And through covetousness shall they with feigned words make merchandise of you: whose judgment now of a long time lingereth not, and their damnation slumbereth not.

Whilst searching through the Internet the other day, in regards to this same subject, this is what I found;

"There are simply no short cuts to the blessings that the Bible speaks of - If we are to know the blessings of God we must follow the ways of God as set out in the Scriptures. Amongst many other things, the Bible is our financial handbook which contains the methods that God has ordained we should handle all of our financial dealings."

There is a large obligation for every Christian to be well versed and acquainted with the Bible. If we are seeking financial blessings in particular, we need to know what the Bible says about finances. People think that ignorance is bliss; in the Kingdom of God, ignorance will kill you, so we must be resolved to seek and understand God's financial systems and laws.

If your faith is weak for finances, a good question to ask yourself is how many Scriptures on finances have you noted? The Bible in several places refers to the words as seeds, and as we become knowledgeable of the Bible through reading, meditating, listening and memorizing, the Bible refers to this process as sowing seeds.

How can someone call himself a pastor yet misguide his Church members to this extent? This kind of person is worse than a sniper or an armed robber; Like many others, his lips are hasty to preach that the Bible says you should not judge a man of God. The last time I saw Benny Hinn lift up his right hand and say, "Curse be any man who says anything bad against me. I want all such curses, I need them, I am hungry for them. Look brothers and sisters, let no man intimidate you, when a man becomes born again, he becomes new in Spirit. The Spirit of Christ dwells in him, and now he is become Christ in a spirit bod, so no witch or wizard could curse him now that he is in Christ and Christ is in him. The will of God will alone come to pass in his life, in God's own time. Do not let the trick of the devil instill fear upon you and distract you from questioning his evil deeds. It is high time the children of God stand in the light of God's Word, which is Jesus Christ, and remain steadfast in His wisdom and promises in your life.

A pastor is someone who exercises spiritual guidance over a number of people and has the obligation to feed them with the right spiritual food. A pastor is not supposed to feed the people with foods that contain little or no nutrients at all, or food that contain toxic substances capable of destroying the spiritual body of the hearers, or alter the spiritual body's healthy growth. A pastor is like a shepherd. You do not expect a shepherd to feed his sheep with papers instead of grass, but it is shameful that numerous big names on television are doing just that. Jesus Christ said something about a shepherd in John 10:11-15 that will help give us a better understanding of what I am trying to say.

11 I am the good shepherd: the good shepherd giveth his life for the sheep.

12 But he that is an hireling, and not the shepherd, whose own the sheep are not, seeth the wolf coming, and leaveth the sheep, and fleeth; and the wolf catcheth them, and scattereth the sheep.

13 The hireling fleeth, because he is an hireling, and careth not for the sheep.

14 I am the shepherd, and know my sheep, and am known of mine.

15 As the Father knoweth me, even so know I the Father: and I lay my life for the sheep.

Jesus said that He is the Good Shepherd and the Good Shepherd gives His life for the sheep. I am not saying that you should die for the sheep, because that was done for us once and for all by the Master himself. Therefore, we are not expected to do that any longer, but by love, our actions should resemble in every way that of Jesus Christ. It is our place to find out the innumerable great things Jesus Christ did, most of which are not even recorded in the Bible from the accounts of the New Testament. Jesus tells us in verses 12 and 13 that hirelings exist, people with self-centered intentions.

To better grasp Jesus' message, you must understand the definition of the term hireling. A hireling is a person who works only for pay, especially in a menial or boring job, with little or no concern for the value of the work. A hireling works only for the material reward. There is no heart or love in the job. He flees when the wolf or thief comes to steal the flock or he betrays his own to gain what satisfies him. Brothers, where is your love for the job you are called to do? This job is not a menial job, it is an honoring job. According to the Lord God Almighty's definition, not all are called, only privileged ones. It is the reason for which the Good One laid down His life. Brethren, you have allowed the devil to rob you of this feeling of love. Don't let your heart of stone overwhelm. The Bible says in 1 Timothy 6:10;

10 For the love of money is the root of all evil: which while some coveted after, they have erred from the faith, and pierced themselves through with many sorrows.

They have pierced themselves with many sorrows, oh what a pity! The thing is, most of these people whose minds are bent on dubbing the children of God with twisted up words from the Bible, will always tell you, thou should not judge so that you will not be judged John 7: 24 says;

24 Judge not according to the appearance, but judge righteous judgment.

Judgment is simply expressing your opinion about something and there is nothing wrong with that. God has never ever said we should not judge. God says we should judge, but in a righteous way, with a positive, lovely and Godly mindset. This is what Paul did in Galatians 2:11-14 and God found no wrong in it. He did not send down terrible curses on Paul, because He who is all knowing knew that Paul was speaking in good faith and for the good of the Body of Christ.

11 But when Peter was come to Antioch, I withstood him to the face, because he was to be blamed.

12 For before that certain came from James, he did eat with the gentiles: but when they were come, he withdrew and separated himself, fearing them which were of the circumcision.

13 And the other Jews dissembled likewise with him; insomuch that Barnabas also was carried away with their dissimulation.

14 But when I saw that they walked not uprightly according to the truth of the gospel, I said unto Peter before them all, If thou, being a Jew, livest after the manner of the gentiles, and not as do the Jews, why compelest thou the Gentiles to live as do the Jews?

to the truth of the gospel, I said unto Peter before them all, If thou, being a Jew, livest after the manner of Gentiles, and not as do the Jews, why compellest thou the Gentiles to live as do the Jews?

I do not hate these men, nor the innumerable others out there, but I do hate the devil in their inside that speaks through them ravaging the God body. I pray that the grace of God will flourish, and touch them within for a positive change. They have allowed the devil to destroy the name of God and the lives of Christians, not sparing even their own Soul. How can you choose that path and not see what has taken ownership of you? Listen and you will hear it, that cry from the spirit man within, saying enough is enough, stop deceiving my people, robbing them of their money and still lead them on the wrong path.

NOTES AND REFLECTIONS FOR READERS

JET PLANE MEN

I have always pondered why a man of God would own five, two or even one private jet. No matter what their justifications are, it is abominable considering how costly these air vessels are. There is no valid justification, especially for men with black skin living in Africa. They have lived to see with their own naked eyes the level of poverty in Africa and how common people die of hunger every day. There are refugees, scattered everywhere and the deadly Ebola virus which was introduced by man to destroy man, all for greed. Considering all these hardships, lack and want experienced by some less priviledged people, and or victimized people, I frown to think of the money wasted on unnecessary luxury objects. I did some research on Google to see how much these jets actually cost; shocking and overwhelming results is what I got.

Allegations of extravagant living among Nigeria's Pentecostal preachers have deepened following the gift of a private jet to the President of the Christian Association of Nigeria. The multi-million dollar jet, a 10-seater with a range of 3,900 nautical miles, was presented to Ayo Oritsejafor by members of his congregation, Word of Life Bible Church, located in Warri. The gift celebrated the pastor's birthday and his 40th anniversary in ministry. Oritsejafor, who also serves as the President of the Pentecostal Fellowship of Nigeria, joins a growing list of preachers with private jets in the West African nation, which is Africa's largest oil producer.

David Oyedepo, the founder of Living Faith Church, also known as Winners' Chapel, is reported to be the richest pastor in Nigeria. He owns three Gulfstreams plus a Learjet worth almost US$100 million. By contrast, Oritsejafor's Bombardier Challenger jet is worth less than US$5 million. Enoch Adeboye, general overseer of the Redeemed Christian Church of God, also owns a private jet. So does the flamboyant founder of Christ Embassy Church, Chris Oyakhilome. Apart from preachers, only top business tycoons, and a few governors and politicians own private jets in a nation where more than 70 percent live on less than US$1 per day. Nigeria's wealthy have spent US$6.5 billion on private jets in the last five years, making it Africa's biggest market for private planes. The number of privately-owned aircrafts rose by 650 percent between 2007 and 2012, up from 20 to 150 planes at an average cost of US$50 million.

Sadly, most Christians in Africa's most populated nation remain poor. Gideon Para-Mallam, regional secretary of the International Fellowship of Evangelical Students, said such preachers are setting bad examples. "This represents another minus to Christianity in a country riddled with much corruption," he said. "We are simply displaying the rottenness of what has become of Nigeria. It is so sad."

Jeremiah Gado, president of the 3 million-strong Evangelical Church Winning All, agrees. "Having a private jet is a distraction and an indication of the lack of unity in the body," he affirms.

Oritsejafor defends the gift maintaining that his private jet is a necessity not a luxury. "Sometimes, my schedule is so complicated," he said at a press conference. "Now, I can move. I can even go and come back home. It is a bit more convenient for me, and I suspect that this is one of the reasons a lot of these other preachers have planes." Oritsefajor has his defenders. To Wale Oke, National Vice President of the Pentecostal Fellowship of Nigeria, a jet is just a tool for faster evangelization. "How can Ayo Oritsejafor, who has to minister around the globe, pastor a very large congregation in Warri and attend to critical national matters in Abuja cope if he has to keep waiting at the airports, in a system where nothing is predictable?" He maintains that Pentecostal preachers will buy more jets to cope with expanding ministries. "They ain't seen anything yet! More of us will yet buy and maintain our jets because, by the mercy of God, we have been given the wisdom to do so."

My beloved Naija, we must say no to these men. We have bred a lot of them, more than any other country in Africa, financing them Heavily. In world ranking, we are second, if not first, and we have fanned the flames of these members far and wide. It is high time we say NO. This evil happens not only in Africa, but the world at large. Of course America's Copeland and many hundreds more are among the greedy flying pastors. In one of his messages, Kenneth Copeland told his congregation that the Lord wants him to confess the billion flow. When he was in the million flow, he was winning millions, so by going into the billion flow, he will win billions. The people responded with an Amen. Let us be honest here, since when in the Bible has money ever been associated with the salvation of the lost? Never! This is a blatant lie and blasphemy at its worst. This man also said that his million dollar jet was to be used for God's purpose, sharing the truth around the world. People, these men are blatant, heartless liars having no iota of truth in them. So how then can they speak it? They are partners and friends working together, birds of the same flock. Research their backgrounds and you will come to the same conclusion. I plead with Christians worldwide to join me in the great outcry. Let us join hands to expose this evil of deceit and manipulation, that the body of Christ might know peace. Pray hard and fast ceaselessly for the mercy and grace of God that the true gospel may overpower and be brought to the hearing of every person of every nation and color. If God is on our side, He is all we need. God, please hear my plea, I beg you to rescue your children. Enough is enough, we can't bear it anymore, so we will wait on you alone to take the lead and do your thing.

Brothers, when I went to convert forty million dollars, the average cost price of a single classy jet to franc cfa, I got twenty billion seven hundred and fifty two million three hundred and eighty six thousand francs. This money can save the lives of millions of people dying from hunger in Africa. Tell me, which portrays the love of God more, to save these poor starving people or to buy an aircraft? This is what Jesus was trying to teach us in the parable of the Good Samaritan. I pray we change our ways in Jesus' name.

Notes and Reflections for Readers

NOTES AND REFLECTIONS FOR READERS

WHAT GOD SAYS
ABOUT YOU GUYS

Mathew 23:1-39;
1 Then spake Jesus to the multitude, and to the disciples,

2 Saying The scribes and the Pharisees sit in Moses' seat:

3 All therefore whatsoever they bid you observe, that observe and do; but do not ye after their works: for they say, and do not.

4 For they bind heavy burdens and grievous to be borne, and lay them on men's shoulders; but they themselves will not move them with one of their fingers.

5 But all their works they do for to be seen of men: they make broad their phylacteries, and enlarge the borders of their garments,

6 And love the uppermost rooms at feasts, and the chief seats in the synagogues,

7 And greetings in the markets, and to be called of men, Rabbi, Rabbi

8 But be not ye called Rabbi: for one is your master, even Christ; and all ye are brethren.

9 And call no man your father upon the earth : for one is your Father, which is in heaven.

10 Neither be ye called masters: for one is your master, even Christ.

11 But he that is greatest among you shall be your servant.

12 And whosoever shall exalt himself shall be abased; and he that shall humble himself shall be exalted.

13 But woe unto you, scribes and Pharisees, hypocrites! For you shut up the kingdom of heaven against men: for ye neither go in yourselves, neither suffer ye them that are entering to go in.

14 Woe unto you, scribes and Pharisees, hypocrites! For ye devour widows' houses, and and for a pretence make long prayer:

15 Woe unto you, scribes and Pharisees, hypocrites! For ye compass sea and land to make one proselyte, and when he is made, ye make him twofold more the child of hell than yourselves.

16 Woe unto you, ye blind guides, which say, whatsoever shall swear by the temple, it is nothing: but whosoever shall swear by the gold of the temple, he is the debtor!

17 Ye fools and blind: for whether is greater, the gold, or the temple that sactifieth the gold?

18 And, whosoever shall swear by the alter, it is nothing; but whosoever sweareth by the gift that is upon it he is guilty.

19 Ye fools and blind: for whether is greater, the gift or the alter that sanctifieth the gift?

20 Whoso therefore shall swear by the alter, swearethby it, and by all things thereon.

21 And whosoever shall swear by the temple sweareth by it, and by him that dwealth therein.

22 And he that shall swear by heaven, sweareth by the throne of God, and by him that sitteth thereon

23 Woe unto you, scribes and Pharisees hypocrites! For ye pay tithe of mint and anise and cummin and have omitted the weightier matters of the law, judgment, mercy, and faith: these ought ye to have done, and not to leave the other undone.

24 Ye blind guides, which strain at a gant, and swallow a camel.

25 Woe unto you, scribes and Pharisees, hypocrites ! for you make clean the outside of the cup and of the platter, but within they are full of extortion and excess.

26 Thou blind Pharisee, cleanse first that which is within the cup and platter, that the outside of them may be clean also.

27 Woe unto you, scribes and Pharisees, hypocrites! For ye are like unto whited sepulchers, which indeed appear beautiful outward, but are within full of dead men's bones, and of all uncleanness.

28 Even so ye also outwardly appear righteous unto men, but within are full of hypocrisy and iniquity.

29 Woe unto you, scribes and Pharisees, hypocrites! Because ye build the tombs of the prophets, and garnish the sepulchers of the righteous,

30 And say, if we had been in the days of our fathers, we would not have been partakers with them in the blood of the prophets.

31 Wherefore ye be witnesses unto yourselves, that ye are the children of them which killed the prophets.

32 Fill ye up then the measure of your fathers.

33 Ye serpents, ye generation of vipers, how can ye escape damnation of hell?

34 Wherefore, behold, I send unto you prophets, and wise men, and scribes: and some of them shall ye scourge in your synagogues, and persecute them from city to city:

35 That upon you may come all the righteous blood shed upon the earth, from the blood of righteous Abel unto the blood of Zacharias son of Barachias, whom ye slew between the temple and the altar.

36 Verily I say unto you, All these things shall come upon this generation.

37 O Jerusalem, Jerusalem, thou that killest the prophets, and stonest them which are sent unto thee, how often would I have gathered thy children together, even as a hen gathereth her chickens under her wings, and ye would not!

38 Behold, your house is left unto you desolate.

39 For I say unto you, ye shall not see me henceforth, till ye shall say, Blessed is he that cometh in the name of the Lord.

Mathew 24:1-2;

1 And Jesus went out, and departed from the temple: and His disciples came to him for to shew him the buildings of the temple.

2 And Jesus said unto them, see ye not all these things? Verily I say unto you, There shall not be left here one stone upon another, that shall not be thrown down.

This is what God is saying to you preachers of today. Descendants of scribes and Pharisees, take special note of Matthew 24:1-2. Depart and turn away from your evil ways; repent and preach the message of the Cross and grace and love, and it shall be well with you. He that has ears, let him listen.

Some months ago a friend that lives in Rome told me in the course of our discussion that brother you know I have been thinking over and over about the things you told me in our last discussion and I even stopped going to the catholic church too, in fact I have been asking God persistently to open my eyes, that I may see some things going on, and God has been showing me some things in revelations. He told me a lot of them, but I will like to share just one of them. He said he saw very big fire that started at the main catholic church in Rome, where the pope is, spreading to other parts of Europe, and extending to Africa and America. One might tempted to think that this fire talked of here is a physical one that will expand to the other parts of the earth causing physical destruction to human beings. No such a fire stands for spiritual death that comes about by the doctrines and traditions of men that has replaced the true word of God, that has its seat and roots in Rome, and has been spreading to other parts of the world.

NOTES AND REFLECTIONS FOR READERS

NOTES AND REFLECTIONS FOR READERS

SEED SOWING IN THE NEW TESTAMENT

In this portion of our work, I will like us to examine a very peculiar portion of the bible, in which Christ, in one of his parables, brings to light, the true seed, that was shadowed in the old testament, Luke 8:1-15;

1 And it came to pass afterward, that he went throughout every city and village, preaching and shewing the glad tidings of the kingdom of God: and the twelve were with him,

2 And certain women, which had been healed of evil spirits and infirmities, Mary called Magdalene, out of whom went seven devils,

3And Joanna the wife of Chuza Herod's steward, and Susanna, and many others, which ministered unto him of their substance.

4 And when much people were gathered together, and were come to him out of every city, he spake by parable:

5 A sower went out to sow his seed: and as he sowed, some fell by the way side; and it was trodden down, and the fowls of the air devoured it.

6 And some fell upon a rock; and as soon as it was sprung up, it withered away because it lacked moisture.

7And some fell among thorns; and the thorns sprang up with it and choked it.

8And other fell on good ground, and sprang up, and bare fruit an hundredfold. And when he had said these things, he **CRIED,** he that hath ears to hear, let him hear.

9 And his disciples asked him, saying, what might this parable be?

10 And he said, unto you it is given to hear the mysteries of the kingdom of God: but to others in parables; that seeing they might see not, and hearing they might not understand.

11 Now the parable is this: the seed is the word of God.

12 Those by the way side are they that hear; then cometh the devil and taketh away the word out of their hearts, lest they should believe and be saved.

13 They on the rock are they, which, when they hear receive the word with joy; and these have no root, which for a while believe and in time of temptation fall away.

14 And that which fell among thorns are they which, when they have heard, go forth and are choked with cares and riches and pleasures of this life, and bring no fruit to perfection.

15 But that on the good ground are they which in an honest and good heart, having heard the word, keep it and bring forth fruit with patience.

This is the sowing of seeds in the New as we get from the coded words of Christ himself. The burden of sowing of seeds in this era is upon the preachers not upon the people. Why? Because seed in this era is the Word of God not money; it has never been money anyway, but grains of crops as we see in the Bible. We are told by Christ in verse 1 that He went about preaching and showing the glad tidings of the kingdom of God. What are the glad tidings? The glad tidings were that the Old has been fulfilled in the New in the person of Christ, and that we no longer need to struggle with the things of the Old, including such useless payments our Churches request. Christ tells us of the sower who went about sowing his seeds; some fell upon the wayside, some fell upon the rock, some fell upon thorns and some fell upon good ground. It happens today where the good ground is the heart which has been graced by God for reception. The rock, thorns and wayside are hearts which have not been given the grace to understand such mysteries. We see this in verse 10.

The Bible says in Galatians 6:8;

8 For he that soweth to the flesh shall of the flesh reap corruption; but he that soweth to the spirit shall of the spirit reap everlasting life.

What does this mean to you? To me, it means he that concentrates on amassing the things of the flesh will be spiritually empty, and this emptiness will lead to corruption and spiritual death. Whereas he who sows to the Soul, the word of truth, will have his Spirit revitalized, and thus will live the everlasting life of Christ. Seek ye first the kingdom of God and His righteousness and all these things will be added unto you (Matthew 6:33). This portion of the Bible is extremely powerful and worth meditating on over and over again.

The Bible says Corinthians 9:8-12;

8 And God is able to make all grace abound toward you, that ye, always having all sufficiency in all things, may abound to every good work:

9 (As it is written, He hath dispersed abroad; he hath given to the poor: his righteousness remaineth forever.

10 Now he that ministereth seed to the sower both minister bread for your food, and multiply your seed sown, and increase the fruit of your righteousness;)

11 Being enriched in everything to all bountifulness, which causeth through us thanksgiving to God.

12 For the administration of this service not only supplieth the want of the saints, but is abundant also by many thanksgivings unto God.

All these verses are crucial, but I would like to expound more on verses 10 and 11 which are relevant to our subject. One may be tempted to think that Paul was talking about physical seed or money as the prosperity preachers will twist it up to mean, but the seed he was talking about was the Word of God, the same seed Christ was talking about in Luke 8. He that ministereth seed to the sower, both minister bread for your food, and multiply your seed sown. The question here to be asked is who ministereth food to the sower? The spirit is the one that does the ministering, He ministers the seed, bringing to light and understanding to the preacher, the truth and mysteries, hidden in the word of God. The spirit ministers seed to the sower, and He still will multiply the seed you sow and thereby increase the fruits of your righteousness.

Notes and Reflections for Readers

Notes and Reflections for Readers

GIVING IN THIS ERA

After researching all the things I wrote in the previous chapters under Tithing and Sowing of Seeds, one might assume that I am against supporting the Church. No, far from it! I can never be against giving support to the work of God, lest I make myself an enemy to God and His will. There is a way God intends us to give in this new era of grace in Christ Jesus; we are of the New, the Old has passed away and the New has come to stay forever. When you give in the new era, you should be free of expecting a reward, for if our giving expects a prize then it is not Christ like. If our giving is not based on faith and love, then it is not powerful enough to stir God and attract His attention. In the Old, God commanded us to give so that it should be well with us. Our giving, which constituted part of the law, stood to justify us before God for our blessings and protection. Whereas in the New, giving is not for our justification; we are saved from all attacks from the enemy, not because we have given, but because Jesus loves us. Romans 5:8 teaches;

8 But God comandeth his love toward us, in that, while we were yet sinners, Christ died for us.

Therefore our justification is not in that which we offer, but in the free will sacrifice of Christ on the Cross. Our giving should also be free willed with no constrains. I will proceed to explain three levels of giving:

1) **Giving To Support The Work Of God**
2) **Giving To The Poor And Needy**
3) **Giving To Your Enemies**

GIVING TO SUPPORT THE WORK OF GOD

Brethren, let no man deceive you by declaring that God has told him that you must give this or that amount to support the work of God. No amount of money will guarantee God repaying you with His blessings, making you abundant financially or free you from an affliction. Such pressure is not of God but of the devil. Indeed, a preacher's dependency should not be on the people, for the people did not call him to service. If they had, he would be operating on a no faith arena, and then how would he be able to please God and stir His guidance? It is normal that in the law of agency, he (the principal) who sends someone (the agent) on an errand has the obligation to provide for the means of transportation, lodging and feeding costs, etc. The employer acts in good faith that his employee will successfully complete the task. Brethren, should someone cry more than the bereaved? The lost souls belong to God. The vision is His; you are just His vessel, a trustee. Does an agent strive to finance the affairs of his employer? No need. Neither should you take more than is offered or expect to control your surroundings. Depend on God entirely, you who have been called by Him. Even if you have minimal money to carry out His assignment, I tell you there is enough to suffice. God is wise and provides. Deny your own understanding and wants, and doors will open. Let your eyes and heart be fixed on the Lord God Almighty. As for your needs, they will be met at the right time. By increasing in your knowledge of God and yourself, and accepting your life given task, you will please God. It takes simple faith.

Brethren, forget those people who say they depend highly upon the benevolence of the Church members. They are just showy men who do not know what they are doing or they know the truth but act in guise. While I was in fellowship with Christ Embassy in Milan, I happened to be in Church on the first Sunday of the year. They celebrated part of the tradition of the Old, including tithe and sowing of seeds, which the Church still practiced as first fruit offering. Church members had to give a substantial amount of their monthly earnings as sacrifice to the altar. While this was going on, a member walked forth to give her first fruit offering. The pastor interrupted her and said that the Spirit of God has ministered her, thus her offering is too little. He encouraged her to go back and add what she came to give. This was such a blatant lie and could never be from God. People who persist in carrying on with such doctrines and refuse to let go are experts in mind reading and manipulation. They listen to their senses and not to the Spirit of God, for the Lord God Almighty is not a God of confusion; He is faithful to His every word. The Bible says in 2 Corinthians 9:7

7 Every man according as he purposeth in his heart, so let him give; not grudgingly, or of necessity: for God loveth a cheerful giver.

Paul was addressing the area of 'giving' to support the work of God. Giving without external influence and compulsion of any sort, no matter how good it may seem or be presented. Not all who say they hear the Spirit means they hear from the Spirit of God. The person may be hearing from strange and unholy spirits or hearing from his own man. 2 Corinthians 9:1 begins with these words, "For as touching the ministering to the saints, it is superfluous for me to write to you."

What does it all mean? I will illustrate with an example. While in Leuven, Belgium, I was at Church and I was touched from my Spirit to give fifty euros to the pastor. Actually, that was the only note I had in my wallet, my all, but I felt pressure to give it to the pastor. I tried to resist seeing the pastor had a very nice car and was living more fine than me who at that time was jobless. The more I resisted, the more I felt compelled from within to give. After much reluctance, I finally made up my mind to yield. I stood up after service, went to the pastor and told him that the Lord told me to give him all that I have; the fifty euros in my wallet. He greatly thanked me as tears ran down his cheek. He shivered, gazed at me in awe then said that things were financially difficult for him at present. He had been out of work for months and he was sharing an apartment with two other people who expected his portion of the house rent today. Before leaving the house, he went down on his knees and prayed earnestly that God would do something to complete his share of the house rent which was short of fifty euros.

God loves a cheerful giver who shares what prospers in his heart. A wise man should communicate with the invisible Man in his Spirit, the still voice of Christ from within. When men of God put their full trust in God alone, He will certainly meet up with their needs timely. He will lead men to minister material things to us at His time. Through their soft words and actions, we shall understand God more and grow in faith. There is no need to talk to people for hours convincing them with manly wisdom or twisting up good intended Scriptures to suit our foolish intentions. Whether this challenges you or not, what I speak is the truth and there is no negotiation. To walk with God, you must trust Him not your own wisdom and ignorance of men. He who walks this path has God on his side full time. His destiny may be slow to be fulfilled, but he should rest assure that in the fullness of God's time, he will burst like a grain of corn releasing itself from the life that was once motionless. What have you to say? Are you more eager to recognize a God given dream than the true Owner of the dream? If you select your own mischievous means to achieve the dream, then be sure to know that you are on your own, for God does not play games or engage in wrongdoing. You can be good at talking your way through and getting money out of people, but that does not secure your success. It only highlights your failure in relation to your calling and walk with God. You have become a rich failure, so to say.

Let us recall the story of King Saul in the Bible. With impatience and failure to wait on God, he forced his own way through to obtain what was rightly set aside for David, God's own true man. The day Saul sought his own wisdom and impatience, he was alone and not with God. Though he still operated as king in the physical realm, he was no king in the realm of the Spirit. He was just a shadow.

Are you a Christian who knows very little of your position in Christ? Beware, because that would make you vulnerable to spiritual rascals. Enjoy life, but avoid putting your trust in vain things. Why travel far and wide for spiritual upkeep when you have the Master Himself dwelling within you. Some years ago, I travelled to Europe on foot through the desert when God told me in a dream to make a move for the way is now open. I passed through Calabar in Nigeria and visited T.B Joshua's Church. To my surprise, I saw people trampling over each other as they scrambled to buy the anointed water. Stop chasing and open your eyes to the bitter truth. That so called anointed water is not anointed by God. Only T.B Joshua knows where it's coming from and he won't tell us. He is a horoscope spiritual business man, making millions of naira from the sales of such items. Turn to the Lord God Almighty. Seek to know Him more and more daily, this is the only way forward.

In the same light, I would like to use an example to illustrate the second portion of 2 Corinthians 9:7 which states, "Not grudgingly, or of necessity: for God loveth a cheerful giver." A new national chairman introduced a system of money offerings in an envelope. On the envelope, the Church member writes their name and how much they are donating. The pastor's reason for doing this was to calculate their weekly donations because they were running short, and had to meet up with the payments of rent, light, water and other bills. I disagreed with this idea because I understood 2 Corinthians 9:7. Whilst every person took an envelope and put in an offering as instructed, I went up and gave my offering. The following Sunday, the pastor announced that no one is to give money by hand, just place it in the envelope. I knew he was talking about me. I was heartbroken and did not give offering that Sunday. I did not appreciate the fact that people would feel obliged to give more than they can afford, because it is recorded. A donation should be optional and anonymous if one wishes. In fact, God makes this secret and serious when He says in Mathew 6:1-4;

1 Take heed that you do not do your charitable deed before men to be seen by them. Otherwise you have no reward from your father in heaven.

2 Therefore, when you do your charitable deed, do not sound a trumpet before you as the hypocrites do in the synagogues and in the

streets, that they may have glory from men. Assuredly I tell you they have their reward.

3 But when you do a charitable deed, do not let your left hand know what your right hand is doing,

4 That way your charitable deeds may be in secret; and your Father who sees in secret will himself reward you openly.

We all know that when the right hand gives, of course the left hand will know since they are of the same body. This was just a hyperbole by Christ to stress the intensity of His seriousness as to how secret our giving in this era should be. Our Heavenly Father who sees our good works in secret will reward us in secret. The Bible says in 1 Timothy 5:17-18;

17 Let the elders that rule well be counted worthy of double honor especially they who labor in the word and doctrine.

18 For the scripture saith, thou shalt not muzzle the ox that treadeth out the corn. And, the labourer is worthy of his reward.

There is a spiritual way of approaching this without being forcefully instructed. Best you communicate with the innermost Man to guide you.

GIVING TO THE POOR AND NEEDY

James 2:15-16

15 If a brother or sister is naked and destitute of daily food,

16 And one of you says to them, "Depart in peace, be warmed and filled" but you do not give them the things which are needed for the body, what does it profit?

Our giving should not stem from a heart of greed, but from a heart of love and compassion. What do I mean by our giving stemming from a heart of greed? Many times, we give because we are manipulated by so called pastors who inform us that they are raising money for this or that project. They even dare to say that God has seen people struggle with financial issues and those who are bold enough to challenge God should come forward and make a huge pledge. By doing this, God will devour their crisis and open all financial doors. Brothers, I tell you, your giving is not out of love, but out of greed. You are like a man who has invested in a business and is waiting for his profits. What do you do when you bypass desolate men starving to death on the streets? Which is more the love of God, to save someone who is dying or give your money to your pastor as tithe or seed? Obviously giving to the needy is a true act of love with no reason to expect a reward. Our giving should stem from a heart of love like that of the Good Samaritan who attended to someone who had been attacked by armed robbers and was severely wounded, left to die. The Bible tells us that the Good Samaritan had enough compassion to approach the helpless man, treat his wounds by pouring oil and wine, bandaged him and brought him to an inn to take care of him. Upon departure, he gave part payment for his treatment and promised to give more if needed.

Compassion is a feeling of deep sympathy and sorrow for another who is stricken by misfortune, accompanied by a strong desire to alleviate their suffering. This is the same virtue that stirred up Jesus when He went about doing the good things He did on earth, to fulfil His mission. This is the same virtue that moved the Good Samaritan. Our giving should resemble that of the Good Samaritan.

Proverbs 19:17

17 He that hath pity upon the poor lendeth unto the Lord; and that which he hath given will he pay him again.

A close friend of mine back in Cameroon took me to visit her sister who had given birth. The bike man charged us three hundred francs instead of the usual two hundred and fifty francs, because the road was bad and it took longer to reach our destination. I understood, but my friend insisted that he give back the fifty francs. Come rain come sun, I pleaded with her but to no avail; she succeeded in collecting the fifty francs from the guy. Later, I explained to her why I was keen for the man to keep the fifty francs. The road was muddy and indeed bad after a severe rainfall. She said that people who release the little money they have will never become rich, but my understanding was different as written in Proverbs 23:4. "Labour not to be rich: cease from thine own wisdom." Proverbs 10:22 says, "The blessing of the LORD, it maketh rich, and he addeth no sorrow with it." These two verses teach that we should not strive in our own abilities and wisdom to be rich, but rather we should trust the Lord, and in due season, He will bless us according to His riches in glory.

Galatians 6:7-9

7 Be not deceived, God is not mocked: for whatsoever a man soweth, that shall he reap also.

8 For he that soweth to the flesh shall of the flesh reap corruption; but he that soweth to the spirit, shall of the spirit reap life everlasting.

9 And let us not be weary in well doing: for in due season we shall reap, if we faint not.

Deuteronomy 15: 7-8

7 If there be among you a poor man of one of thy brethren within any of thy gates in thy land which the Lord thy God giveth thee, thou shalt not harden thy heart nor shut thine hand from thy poor brother:

8 But thou shalt open thine hand wide unto him, and shalt surely lend him sufficient for his need, in that which he wanteth

In Isaiah 58:6-11, God told the Israelites;

6 Is not this the fat that I have chosen? To loose the bands of the wickedness, to undo the heavy burdens, and to let the oppressed go free, and that ye break every yoke?

7 Is it not to deal thy bread to the hungry, and that thou bring the poor that are cast out to thy house? When thou seest the naked, that thou cover him; and that thou hide not thine self from thy own flesh?

8 Then shall thy light break forth as the morning, and thine health shall spring forth speedily: and thy righteousness shall go before thee; the glory of the lord shall be thy reward.

8 Then shall thy light break forth as the morning, and thine health shall spring forth speedily: and thy righteousness shall go before thee; the glory of the Lord shall be thy reward.

9 Then shalt thou call upon the Lord and he shall answer you, thou shall cry and he shall say, here I am. If thou take away from the midst of thee the yoke, the putting forth of the finger and speaking vanity;

10 And if thou draw out thy soul to the hungry, and satisfy the afflicted soul, then shall thy light rise in obscurity, and thy darkness be as the noon day:

11 And the Lord shall guide thee continually, and satisfy thy soul in drought, and make fat thy bones: and thou shalt be like a watered garden, and like a spring of ater, whosewaters fail not.

Brethren, in line with this portion of the Bible, let me share this testimony with you. One day, I slept and had a dream in the middle of the night. In that dream, I saw myself by a river and close to me was a woman sitting on a rock holding her baby son. All of a sudden, the woman called out saying I should loan her some money. The baby stood up on his feet and started speaking, pleading with me to consider the demand of his mother and loan her money because she was in financial need. When the baby finished speaking, I awoke from my sleep. I knew God wanted me to reach out to someone, but whom? I earnestly prayed for God to direct me to the person in need then I went back to sleep. The following morning, I was open to God's direction. During the course of the day, I was communicating with one of my few trustworthy friends, Chi Akuma Roland, on Facebook. In the course of our discussion, I asked after one young man, a prophet who was an orphan. I used to help the guy from time to time financially, but we lost contact. Akuma said that the young man called him earlier that day, all distressed, because he was struggling to pay his school fees. I knew this was the person God wanted me to help, so I requested his number. I called him and he divulged that he was struggling financially and the school proprietor withdrew his scholarship, because he was absent from school for several days whilst evangelizing. I asked him how much he owed, and although I had my own financial problems having lost my job, I placed my trust in God. In fact, I counted myself privileged that God would ask a favour of me, so I sent him the money that same day. That night, I had another dream. This time God came to me and showed me some plagues, but I don't know whether these plagues have passed or are yet to come. As He turned His back to leave, I cried out to Him to deliver me from my constant wet dreams. I was actually suffering from attacks from a succubus spirit that ended with me ejaculating for more than ten years. God turned back, faced me and told me to turn behind and look at the world; I was to take the drama of the world and empty those thoughts. I did, and when I turned towards the front, I saw Jesus on His cross and the Cross was shining like polished brass. When I emptied the thoughts onto the Cross, heavy thunder started striking and heavy rain fell on Christ and His Cross only. Then I saw tears running down His cheeks. Just then God told me it is finished. He turned His back and left, then I got up from my sleep.

Christ says in Mathew 25:34-44;

34 Then shall the king say unto them on his right hand, come, ye blessed of my father, inherit the kingdom prepared for ye from the foundation of the world:

35 For I was an hungred, and ye gave me meat; I was thirsty, and ye gave me drink: I was a stranger, and ye took me in:

36 Naked, and ye clothed me: I was sick, and ye visited me: Was in prison, and ye came unto me.

37 Then shall the righteous answer him, saying, Lord, when saw we thee an hungred, and fed thee? Or thirsty, and gave thee drink?

38 When saw we thee a stranger, and took thee in? or naked, and clothed thee?

39 Or when saw we thee sick, or in prison, and came unto thee?

40 And the king shall answer and say unto them, Verily I say unto you, Inasmuch as ye have done it unto one of the least of these my brethren, ye have done it unto me.

41 Then shall he say also unto them on the left hand, Depart from me, ye cursed, into everlasting fire, prepared for the devil and his angels:

42 For I was an hungred, and ye gave me no meat: I was thirst, and ye gave me no drink:

43 I was an hungred, and ye gave me no meat: I was thirsty, and ye gave me no drink:

43 I was a stranger, and ye took me not in: naked, and ye clothed me not: sick, and in prison, and ye visited me not.

44 Then shall they also answer him, saying, Lord, when saw we thee and hungred, or athirst, or a stranger, or naked, or sick, or in prison, and did not minister unto thee?

Christ makes a more serious point in verse 45

Then shall he answer them, saying, Verily I say unto you, Inasmuch as ye did not to one of the least of these, ye did it not to me.

1 John 4:20 says;

20 If a man say, I love God, and hateth his brother, he is a liar; for he that loveth not his brother whom he hath seen, how can he love God whom he hath not seen?

GIVING TO YOUR ENEMIES

This is the greatest and most powerful of all three. Even when we become born again Christians, you will agree it is still highly difficult to pray for people who mistreat and belittle us. Extending a hand of support towards them when they are in need is challenging enough. This is the unfortunate truth and it takes a truly regenerated person, one who has been blessed with grace in the love and knowledge of Christ, to forgive and move forward. Great Apostle Paul says it is the power of God unto salvation to be able to act in the similitude of Christ. We know Jesus is the beginning and the end of love. He suffered and died on the Cross for us, heartless sinners. The parable of the Good Samaritan that Jesus taught in Luke 10:25-37 is illustrative here. Let us examine it critically as I explain further.

Luke 10: 25-37;

25 And, behold, a certain lawyer stood up, and tempted him, saying Master, what shall I do to inherit eternal life?

26 He said unto Him, what is written in the law? How readest thou?

27 And he answering said, Thou shalt love the lord thy God with all thy heart, and with all thy soul, and with all thy strength, and with all thy mind; and thy neighbor as thyself.

28 And he said unto him, Thou hast answered right: this do and thou shall live.

28 And he said unto him, Thou hast answered right: this do, and thou shalt live.

29 But he, willing to justify himself, said unto Jesus, And who in my neighbor?

30 And Jesus answering said, A certain man went down from Jerusalem to Jericho, and fell among thieves, which stripped him of his raiment, and wounded him, and departed, leaving him half dead.

31 And by chance there came down a certain priest that way: and when he saw him, he passed by on the other side.

32 And likewise a levite, when he was at the place, came and looked on him, and passed by on the other side.

33 But a certain Samaritan, as he journeyed, came where he was: and when he saw him, he had compassion on him,

34 And went to him, and bound up his wounds, pouring in oil and wine, and set him on his own beast, and brought him to an inn and took care of him.

35 And on the morrow when he departed, he took out two pence, and gave them to the host, and said unto him, take care of him; and whatsoever thou spendest more, when I come again, I will repay thee.

36 Which now of these three, thinkest thou, was neighbor unto him that fell among thieves?

37 And he said, He that shewed mercy oh him. Then he said Jesus unto him, go, and do thou likewise.

It is evident that the person moving from Jerusalem to Jericho was a Jew, and we know that the Jews and Samaritans were enemies even before the coming of Christ. The Assyrians took many of the conquered Jews from the Northern Kingdom back to their home country in order to keep an eye on them and prevent rebellion. That left many empty farms, houses and businesses. The king of Assyria brought people from different counties to fill the void and they settled in the region of Samaria. These people did not worship the One God of the Jews, but worshipped many gods. It is a safe assumption to accept that the Jews who had remained in their country intermarried with the newcomers and followed in the same practice. These people did not leave but remained in the land, and most likely continued to intermarry and blend in with the other Jews up to the time of Jesus. They continued their practice of worshipping numerous gods, so you can see why the Jews loathed them.

Jesus was using this parable to tell the Jewish lawyer to love his neighbor, the Samaritan, as himself, and also to emulate the example of the Samaritan who catered for the attacked Jew with compassion. A priest and a Levite who were Jews saw him in need, but passed by without lending a hand, but a Samaritan of all people was the one who reached out to him in a Christ manner.

As we can see from the above Scripture, it does not take titles like priest, Levite, bishop, pope, reverend and archbishop to be attracted to people. Even our enemies are in need. It takes one whose heart has been renewed by grace into the likeness of Christ to see the purity in people. Pray earnestly for this virtue. This was Christ's chief secret.

Mathew 5:43-45;

43 Ye have heard that it hath been said, Thou shalt love thy neighbor, and hate thine enemy.

44 But I say unto you, Love your enemies, bless them that curse you, do good to them that hate you, and pray for them which despitefully use you, and persecute you;

45 That ye may be the children of your father which is in heaven: for he maketh his sun to rise on the evil and on the good, and sendeth rain on the just and the unjust.

Romans 12:20-21;

20 Therefore if thine enemy hunger, feed him; if he thirst, give him drink: for in so doing thou shalt heap coals of fire on his head.

21Be not overcome of evil, but overcome evil with good.

NOTES AND REFLECTIONS FOR READERS

Notes and Reflections for Readers

How God Wants Us To Prosper In This Era

The world's definition of prosperity is achieving financial success. That is not God's definition of prosperity. Yet, the Christian world has fallen for the deception that prosperity means obtaining great financial wealth. Now Christians are trying to become millionaires instead of being content with what they have and seek true spiritual riches. It is these true spiritual riches that the Bible speaks of which we need to seek. What is the Bible's and God's definition of prosperity? It has nothing to do with money, although for some, money might be one manifestation of Biblical prosperity, but certainly not in every case.

God wants you to prosper, but He does not necessarily want you to be financially rich. If some Christians become too wealthy, it could destroy their true spiritual riches if they are not established in the things of God first. Many teach prosperity to mean "having good success" and "without lack," which is correct, then they go on to talk about money, but they preface it with a phrase like, "But prosperity is not just getting financial wealth." Then they go on to talk about financial wealth and how God wants to make you a millionaire. God certainly does not want you to stay in poverty, but He may not necessarily want you financially wealthy, for that could destroy your relationship with Him if you are not a mature Christian. How is it fair that for years you have been giving huge sums of money to your pastor, making him to get richer from a millionaire to a billionaire? Yet he keeps telling you that God is about blessing you. God does not need your money to make you rich; you are only being deceived by your pastor whose spiritual eyes have been blinded by the love of money, and whenever they come across any scripture in the bible all they can see or think of is money, because their whole system has been transformed by that, and that is what they speak, expect nothing else from them because you will never have it. It is high time you open your eyes and join in the great outcry for the lost true Gospel that the people of Old used to enjoy in the days of the Apostles. God is not blind. It is common that wealthy people tend to make poor Christians. Why? They have greater temptation to rely on money and put it first before God. The prosperity God intends for us in the Bible is that of the Soul. We are to grow in the Spirit by the Word before becoming financially prosperous. The Book of 3 John 1:2 says;

3 John1:2;
My dear brother, I hope that you may prosereth in all things,
and be in health, even as thy soul prospereth.

Your prosperity men have twisted the Bible, not sparing any single Scripture, to suit their plot. I will cite two or more examples of twisted Scriptures and their real interpretations as intended for the good of the Godly body.

Proverbs 24:3-5;
3 Through wisdom is an house buided; and by understanding it is established:
4 And by knowledge shall the chambers be filled will all precious and pleasant riches.
5 A wise man is strong; yea, a man of knowledge increaseth strength.

These three verses in Proverbs are talking about the real riches of the Kingdom of God not pitiful measly dollars and gold. "Through wisdom the house is builded" means through the wisdom of Christ, the house, which is the human spirit is established by salvation through faith in Christ. The chambers will be filled with precious and pleasant riches which are the gifts of the spirit, true spiritual riches of a man. We keep lowering God by imagining that He thinks like us. We need to see that what He values is true riches not what we value. True treasure is to know Him, know who you are and live a spiritual life in Him. That is all! It is simple yet so powerful. Knowing God is genuine prosperity, and there is no match to what the teachers are calling prosperity today.

Another example of so-called prosperity teachers taking a verse out of context is 2 Corinthians 8:9;

9 For ye know the grace of our Lord Jesus Christ, that though he was rich, yet for our sakes he became poor, that ye through his poverty might be rich.

Some declare that this verse is saying that Jesus became poor so we could become rich. Then they argue that Jesus was never financially poor, because if He was poor whilst doing His will, then it is hard to believe God would make us rich. So the 'poor' here is referring to spiritually, which is correct. But then they say the 'rich' in this verse is referring to financially which is out of context. The 'poor' and 'rich' have absolutely nothing to do with money. It is talking about Jesus becoming spiritually poor, setting aside His former glory of being God (Spirit) and taking up a human body form. He was ridiculed, badly beaten and nailed to the Cross, so that we could become spiritually rich and put on His righteousness. To say that the 'poor' is spiritual and the 'rich' is financial is incorrect Bible interpretation.

To always be on track in our venture to get the right meaning out of the words of Christ, we should always see from the light of the deep spiritual meaning he conceals by the help of the holy spirit. Outside of this, we are but pitifully staggering through the darkness of our own minds.

Revelation 3:14-19 says;
14 And unto the angel of the church of the Laodiceans write; these things saith the Amen, the faithful and true witness, the beginning of the creation of God;

15 I know thy works, that thou art neither cold nor hot: I would thou wert cold or hot.

16 So then because thou art lukewarm, and neither cold nor hot, I will spue thee out of my mouth.

17 Because thou sayest, I am rich, and increased with goods, and have need of nothing; and knowest not that thou art wretched, and miserable, and poor, and blind, and naked:

18 I counsel thee to buy of me gold tried in the fire, that thou mayest be rich; and white, that thou mayest be clothed and that the shame of thy nakedness do not appear; and anoint thine eyes with eyeslave, that thou mayest see.

19 As many as I love, I rebuke and chasten; be zealous therefore and repent.

Do not be surprised to observe that those who deceive you to get your money are never satisfied no matter how much they receive. Give them the whole world and they will ask for Venus. Give them Venus and they will request the stars. Give them the stars and they will ask for the sky. No evil spirit within can ever be satisfied.

Ecclesiastes 5:10 says;

10 He that loveth silver shall not be satisfied with; nor he that loveth abundance will increase; this is also vanity.

Luke 12:15;

15 And he saitd unto them, take heed, and beware of covetousness: for a man's life consisteth not in the abundance of things which he possesseth.

God is warning you today to stop, be attentive and turn away from deceiving His people. The further they move away from Him, the more you are accountable.

Look brothers and sisters in the Lord, the fact that God tells you in a dream or vision that He has answered your prayers and has opened up closed financial doors in front of you doesn't necessarily mean that you will get up the next day and your financial situation becomes bettered up instantly. God does not work like they do in the occult. Your prayers can be answered today, in the realm of the spirit yet it takes one, two, five, ten years or even more for it to manifest in the physical realm. We often become tempted, to give up the patience, tolerance and endurance when we are over burdened by hardship and extreme rough times. But we should always remember the men in the bible, who had great promises, like Joseph and David, how much they suffered and how long it took for their promised inheritance to come to pass. We have to pray continually for the grace of God to abound in our lives and that he gives us the spirit of patience and endurance to stand strong, when difficult times hit hard persistently on un, lest we fall and regret all the rest of our lives. Remember bible says the crown of glory awaits he that endures to the end. Some people are meant to start experiencing their break trough at thirty, or even lesser, some at forty, some at fifty or even sixty, through their children, however, he that be patient and thankful to God for good health, life and each day's provision, while he waits patiently for the dawn of his own day is the greater man indeed, no matter how small he might be seen in the eyes of men.

I lost a relative, one so dear to me, a friend and companion, who wanted to travel out of the country to hustle but had very little money, and so I advised to go to Equatorial Guinea, I had made almost five years out of the country or more during this time with nothing to show for still waiting at the feet of God patiently, when I was called by my closed relatives, who told me that my friend and brother had returned home, barely one to two years or so that he left the country, and had built a six apartment house, married a wife and was sharing money in the family, and that there were words spreading in the family that I had gone to Europe to sleep. On one particular night after praying for the entire family in one of my midnight prayer sessions, I had a vision in which God was showing me that my brother had joined the occult. In the dream I saw my with some occult men in a meeting, dressed in red, and holding clay pots in their hands full of blood. I got up prayed for my brother, and the next day, I called him to ask him if he had anything to do with the occult for God had showed me that he had dirtied his hands, but he refused, the following day I slept and had the same dream again. A year later or so, I had a call from Cameroon that my brother was dead, that he had serious malaria, some said he had kidney failure. I tried to explain to my sister that all that was not what killed our brother, that he was actually a member of the occult in Equatorial Guinea. The occult group in which he was might have asked him to sacrifice a member of his family and he refused then they inflict him with any kind of sickness, even with mere head ache, causing him severe pain, till he finally succumbs to yield to their demands, if he doesn't, they will finally take his life, that the sickness was not actually what killed him, but a mere cover up. My sister believed me not and said that I am very superstitious that our brother died of sickness and was admitted in the hospital, no matter how I tried to make her understand, she was closed up. Our dear brother was gone before his time. He was almost forty five years of age and had given up waiting for his own appointed time, so he decided to take the short cut, not knowing that he had taken the short cut indeed unto death. That is the way a lot of young guys out there loose their lives joining the occult, in Nigeria most especially, to get rich, after giving up their father, mother, children and other family relations, they still end up being killed themselves. A friend of mine once told me a story of someone who joined the occult very young, sacrificed his mother and sister, and became extremely rich but he lived not to enjoy the blood gotten money. The spirits of his mother and sister kept hunting and tormenting him, molesting him every night. He built a beautiful house but could not live inside because his mother's spirit would hunt him there every night. He kept changing houses from one town to the other but his mother's spirit kept chasing him everywhere he relocated to. He finally died, after consulting numerous native doctors to try and protect him to no avail. He should have contacted but rather a true man of God because only the true light of God can utterly ravage any filth in the dark.

NOTES AND REFLECTIONS FOR READERS

NOTES AND REFLECTIONS FOR READERS

FALSE PREACHERS INTIMIDATE YOU SAYING THOU SHALL NOT JUDGE

You will agree with me that it is false prophets who often teach people the wrong thing and rob them of their money, who in the bid to keep the people from speaking against what they say that have propagated this far, this twisted up portion of the bible. They often recite the Bible Scripture, 'Thou shall not judge.' Judgement is simply giving your opinion about a situation. When we say a piece of paper is brown and not white, we are simply giving our personal opinion and that is judgement. We judge every now and then when we open our mouths to speak. The preacher likewise judges every now and then when he mounts the pulpit to preach. When the preacher, for example, says that Peter stole a piece of meat from the pot, even without saying it is wrong, he has judged Peter already. False prophets and teachers usually claim that they are 'God's anointed.' It is a method of intimidation and a scare tactic. They are indirectly saying that God will curse you if you criticize or expose me. No false prophet is 'God's anointed' or should be left 'untouched' and tolerated for their wrongdoing.

Every Christian is God's anointed! NOT just some prophet. We are all anointed by God if we become born again and accept Jesus Christ as our Savior, because the anointing comes from the Spirit of God which dwells within us. Do not let these false prophets intimidate you. The Bible tells us in Ephesians 5:11, "Have nothing to do with the fruitless deeds of darkness, but rather expose them." Matthew 7:1-6 is often taken out of context to claim that so-called men of God should not be judged by anyone. "Judge not, that you be not judged. For with what judgment you judge, you will be judged; and with the measure you use, it will be measured back to you." It is not referring to specific judgements but rather hypocritical judgements. "And why do you look at the speck in your brother's eye, but do not consider the plank in your own eye? Or how can you say to your brother, Let me remove the speck from your eye; and look, a plank is in your own eye? Hypocrite! First remove the plank from your own eye, and then you will see clearly to remove the speck from your brother's eye. Do not give what is holy to the dogs; nor cast your pearls before swine, lest they trample them under their feet, and turn and tear you in pieces."

NOTE: "First remove the plank from your own eye, and then you will SEE CLEARLY to remove the speck from your brother's eye." First embrace God's wisdom for yourself then you will see clearly what is wrong with others.

John 7:24 Judge not to the appearance, but judge righteous judgement.

2 Timothy 4:2 Preach the word; be instant in season; reprove, rebuke, exhort with all long suffering and doctrine.

Titus 2:15 These things speak, and exhort, and rebuke with all authority. Let no man despise thee.

1 Corinthians 2:15 But he that is spiritual judgeth all things, yet he himself is judged of no man.

2 Timothy 3:16 All scriptures is given by inspiration of God, and is profitable for doctrine, and for reproof, for correction, for instruction in righteousness:

2 Peter: 1-3 says;

2 Peter 2: 1-3 But there were false prophets also among the people, even as there shall be false teachers among you, who privily shall bring in damnable heresies, even denying the Lord that bought them, and bring upon themselves swift destruction. And many shall follow their pernicious ways; by reason of whom the way of the truth shall be evil spoken of. And through covetousness shall they feigned works make merchandise of you: whose judgement now of a long time lingereth not, and their damnation slumbereth not.

Scriptures clearly illustrate in the Bible, both in the Old and New Testament, God has imparted to man the authority to judge: (Leviticus 19:15; Deuteronomy 1:16; Deuteronomy 16:18; Judges 2:16-19; II Chronicles 19:5; Ezra 7:25; Isaiah 1:17; Ezekiel 23:45; John 7:24; Romans 2:27; I Corinthians 2:15; 1 Corinthians 6).

In Zechariah 3:7, God states that He gives those who obey Him the authority to judge, "Thus saith the LORD of hosts; If thou wilt walk in my ways, and if thou wilt keep my charge, then thou shalt also judge my house, and shalt also keep my courts, and I will give thee places to walk among these that stand by."

There are additional references in Scripture to this process of judging that may not specifically use the word judge. For example, in the original languages, the words translated as judge in Scripture are also translated as examine, search, discern, ask, question, contend, esteem and determine. In the Old Testament, God specifically identified those who held the position as Judges over His people in the Book of Judges. We also see that one responsibility of the prophets was to declare God's judgment to the people (Judges 4:4; 2 Samuel 12:1-12; Micah 3:1-8; Malachi 4:4; Hosea 6:5). In Ezra 7:25, it states that those who judge serve two purposes:

1) To judge those who know the law.
2) To teach the law to those who do not know.

Scripture also shows that God considers the exercise of judgement to be evidence of us seeking truth. Judging righteously is highly esteemed by God and this is clearly illustrated in 1 Kings 3:9-13. In verse 9, King Solomon asks, "Give therefore thy servant an understanding heart to judge thy people, that I may discern between good and bad: for who is able to judge this thy so great a people?" We see here that Solomon asked God for discernment to judge between good and bad. This request not only pleased the Lord, but God blessed Solomon greatly for asking for the wisdom to judge.

In the New Testament, we continue to see that God expects us to exercise judgement. Jesus Himself criticised the Pharisees for being unable to judge the spiritual things of God. The importance of judging spiritual matters is continually stressed throughout His disciples' ministries (Matthew 16:3; Luke 12:56-57; John 7:24; Acts 4:19; 1 Corinthians 2:15; 1 Corinthians 5:3; 1 Corinthians 6:2-5; 1 Corinthians 10:15; 1 Corinthians 14:29; Hebrews 5:14). Further, we are told that it is to our shame if there are none among us who can judge the things of God. Our Lord states that judgement is considered as one of the weightier aspects of God's law, even more than offerings (Matthew 23:23; Luke 11:14).

When citing God's 'command' not to judge, people often refer to Matthew 7:1. However, let us look at the complete Scripture in context. Jesus clearly says do not judge so that you will not be judged, but to whom is He speaking? He identifies His audience in verse 5 with the words "Thou hypocrite." Jesus is not forbidding Christians to judge (unless He is calling every Christian a hypocrite). He is warning that we will be held accountable for what we know. In other words, if we know enough about sinful behaviour to tell others that it is wrong, then we should not remain silent and allow sin to be present in our lives. This is consistent with Paul's advice in 1 Corinthians 11:31-32 that we should judge ourselves first so that we will not be judged. As Jesus teaches, we should first cast the beam out of our own eyes then point out the fault of others.

NOTES AND REFLECTIONS FOR READERS

NOTES AND REFLECTIONS FOR READERS

THE GREATEST OF ALL
SPIRITUAL GIFTS

Many people consider 1 Corinthians 13 the most beautiful piece of literature in the New Testament. It is certainly the most beloved. Most couples want to have at least a portion of the chapter read at their weddings. It has often been set to music because of its poetic qualities, but this chapter can be very easily torn out of context. It can become a hymn to romantic love or a sentimental sermon on Christian brotherhood that is not rooted in Biblical reality. We will be saved from that sort of misinterpretation or misapplication if we keep in mind that Chapter 13 is in the flow of Paul's discussion of spiritual gifts. Paul writes at the end of Chapter 12, "But earnestly desire the greater gifts. And I show you a more excellent way." At the beginning of Chapter 14 he says, "Pursue love, yet desire earnestly spiritual gifts..."

In Chapter 13, Paul is dealing with the problem of loveless in the Corinthian Church. They struggled with the abuse of spiritual gifts, division in the Church, envy of other people's gifts, selfishness (they brought lawsuits against each other as brothers and sisters), impatience with one another at public meetings and disgraceful behaviour that dishonoured the Lord himself when they came to celebrate Holy Communion. This chapter teaches us that the only way spiritual gifts can be expressed creatively, effectively, and joyfully is when Christians are motivated by love.

In 1 Corinthians 12:31, after his discussion of gifts, Paul says, "I will show you a more excellent way," and that way is love. In Romans 12:9, right after the discussion of gifts, he says, "Let love be without dishonesty." In Ephesians 4:15, he talks about speaking the truth and building in love. The Apostle Peter, in his general discussion of spiritual gifts says, "And above all things have fervent charity among yourselves: for charity shall cover the multitude of sins." (1 Peter 4:8).

1 Corinthians 13 divides into three sections. In verses 1-3, Paul focuses on the ultimate importance of love in the life of the body. In verses 4-7, he talks about the practice of love or love expressed as an activity. Finally in verses 8-13, he talks about the permanence of love. Let's look at verses 1-3. This section makes a clear point that using spiritual gifts, doing good deeds or even becoming a martyr for the sake of the Gospel has no ultimate value unless it is motivated by love. Love is the context in which these gifts and deeds gain significance. If I speak with the tongues of men and of Angels, but do not have love, I have become a noisy gong or a clanging cymbal. If I have the gift of prophecy, know all mysteries and all knowledge, and if I have all faith, so as to move mountains, but do not have love, I am nothing. If I give all my possessions to feed the poor and if I deliver my body to be burned, but do not have love, it profits me nothing.

Now, the love that is defined throughout the chapter is the word 'Agape.' It is a unique word that the Christian community in the first century adopted for their own specific use. First of all, it defines God's supernatural love. It is the way that God views us and acts towards us. God expressed a deep concern for our well-being when he sent Jesus Christ to die for us. The Cross symbolizes His love and willingness to go all-out for us. God's love is a love of intelligent purpose and unqualified acceptance. It is active on our behalf and spares no expense for the good of the beloved. Now, as we express that love through our own lives, it means that we make deliberate commitments, and involve our mind and will. Love is not just an emotional response; our agape love, like God's, is intelligent and purposeful. It is not passive; it involves making decisions that commit us to a policy that is not dictated by emotions. It is a commitment to act for the highest good of the other, whether that person deserves it or not, whether they respond to us or not. Exercising love can be wonderfully accompanied by all kinds of warm feelings and it can be a victory over negative feelings.

Now let us look closely at these three verses. This kind of agape love is absolutely necessary. Paul reviews some of the spiritual gifts that we looked at in Chapter 12 and shows their emptiness apart from love. Verse 1 speaks of eloquent communication, but Paul says without love it counts as nothing. If the gift of tongues is exercised without the motivation of agape, this expression of worship to God is reduced to little more than an empty pagan ritual. Even the most gifted Christian orator, who is positively angelic in his powers of communication, will be spiritually superficial apart from the power of love at work through his eloquence.

In most of the pagan temples in Corinth, there would be large gongs or cymbals hanging at the entrance. As the worshipers came in, they would bang them to attract the attention of the gods, so the gods would respond. Paul's point in using this illustration, which would have been familiar to the Corinthians, is that this was the typical expression of the gift of tongues. The most moving Christian eloquence, without love, is nothing more than an empty pagan rite. Communication without love is a useless thing no matter how effective the communicator.

Verse 2 tells us that knowledge and power without love are nothing. He mentions three more spiritual gifts from Chapter 12: Prophecy, Knowledge and Faith. Remember, we saw that prophecy is a speaking gift. This is a strong challenge to anyone who tries to deal with the Scriptures as a Biblical scholar, theologian or preacher, because it reminds us that the power behind what we do lies in the motivation. If we are driven by self-interest, and the desire for praise or promotion, then our influence as teachers is going to be undercut. No matter how orthodox or persuasive our words are, love should be the energy. Even the important gift of faith and vision, that Paul mentions, must be controlled by love for other people. If I am cantankerous or hard to get along with, even though I can move mountains by faith in God's wonder-working ability, exercising that gift is an absolute zero from God's perspective.

Paul goes on to talk about 'giving' in verse 3. The Jews prized the giving of alms to the poor as a religious act and the early Christians picked up the idea. This challenge must have been a severe blow to the believers in Corinth who were all puffed-up about their generous alms-giving, but failed to love one another. Paul also makes the point that sacrifice to the point of martyrdom, without love, is nothing. When sacrifice is motivated by self-interest and pride, it loses its spiritual value and gains no special heavenly credit.

Pure love is the solution, brethren. If our whole system was filled with true love, there would be no space for the devil to lure us into robbing our beloved and extort money from them. Rather, we would be fighting with the last drop of our blood, sacrificing our lives to defend their Souls from the attacks of hell.

Notes and Reflections for Readers

NOTES AND REFLECTIONS FOR READERS

THE WAY OUT

Several months ago, I was on the tram, on my way to visit my close friend, Obale Stanley. An Arab guy sat opposite me and my Spirit Man was persistent that I preach to Him. I did not know how to initiate conversation, so I silently asked my Spirit Man what I should say to this stranger. There and then, I felt inspired to ask him if he was in search of the truth in regards to which spiritual path to follow. He said yes, looked at me closely then took a deep breath which made me sense he was worried over this issue. I told him that Jesus Christ is the way, the truth and the life. (John14:6). Any path away from Christ is false. I was shocked at his response, enough to break my heart. He questioned how I could expect him to believe in a God that was dead. I enquired where he got such information from and he told me he read it in a book written by a renowned professor in South Africa. To him, Christians are very stupid to believe and worship someone who is dead. How traumatizing to hear that such pessimism is fed to people with faith. God (Christ) is alive. He is Spirit, He is invisible and He is intangible. He is like the air we breathe. He only took the form of a man coming through His earthly Mother Mary to fulfil His divine mission of offering Himself to die on the Cross, to redeem man from the consequences of sin. Mary was not impregnated by Joseph the "earthly father" of Jesus. She conceived by the power of the Holy Spirit. Do not be deceived brethren, Jesus Christ is the one and only way to the Father, ALL other ways are FALSE. He is the King of kings and the Lord of lords. At the mention of His name, every knee bows. His name is more powerful than any other name. This is why it is forbidden to mention that name in any occult gathering, because the mention of that name causes havoc in any evil assembly.

I first saw the power of that name manifested in my presence fifteen years ago. I was not born again yet. I was in a taxi with my aunt who was also not born again. Our car was passing a curve on a hill in Bamenda, Cameroon and there was a big lorry camping on the other side. We were about to collide with the lorry, but in the twinkle of an eye, the driver swiftly curved to the left then to the right. There was a deep valley by the side, but our car did not go inside. If it had gone into the valley, we would most likely not be here today. Many times in my dreams, I have been taken to occult meetings to be introduced or killed, but when I mention the name of Jesus Christ, the whole place starts to shake like an earthquake then I am let out. This is how occult men kill a lot of people, first in the Spirit then it becomes real. In another dream, a close friend took me to such a meeting. When we got inside the house, I saw everyone in red garments and they were doing some incantations. My friend wore his own red garment and was about to present me with one when I rushed in front of them and yelled a severe warning. I then rushed out of the house and I said in the mighty name of Jesus Christ, let this building fall down flat. It did and there was no single block left. I started walking off when a member tried to attack me. I said in the mighty name of Jesus Christ, may you disappear, and he vanished immediately. Then I got up from my sleep.

Jesus is the only way out. The Book of John 10:9 says

John 10: 9 says;

9 I am the door: by me if any man enter in, he shall be saved, and shall go in and out, and find pasture.

Christ is the door. To get into a house, you must go through the door. To get to the throne of God, you must go through Jesus Christ. He is the free access. He did not say that He and Buddha, or any other person, are the doorway to the Father. Christ has set us permanently free from the power and consequences of sin by His grace, which means it is a free gift. We do need to rely on our own works or abilities for our salvation, but we do need to rely on the grace of God alone. It is as free as the air we breathe, but if we do not know it or cherish it, we are doomed and trapped in the webs of impostors who try to bottle air and sell it to us. Christianity is based on faith and is in the knowing.

John 8:32
32 And ye shall know the truth, and the truth shall make you free.

It is the knowledge of the truth that sets us free. Paul says in Romans 1:16 that he is not ashamed of the Gospel of Christ. It is the power of God unto salvation to every man that believes. We are saved by the power of this Gospel and that alone, if only we can trust.

Many believe that those who have the Holy Spirit are immune from demonic bondage. This theology usually stems from a faulty belief that the mind and Soul are the same things. The moment we are born again, our Souls are reborn and the Holy Spirit is united with our Soul. The mind of a man is not instantly reborn as the Spirit is. Our minds are where the dirt lies and where the demon dwells not our Spirits. Therefore, there is no reason to believe that a Christian is immune from demonic bondage, because their minds are usually on the dirty side until they are renewed over time, as the transformation does not happen instantly. If the mind and Spirit were the same things, you would instantly be a perfect person, never to sin again once you are born again. There would be no sin or dark thoughts roaming within, no desire to do wrong, and you would bitterly hate immorality, because your mind is perfectly united with God, therefore there would be no room to sin. In John 8:31-34, Jesus tells us that even though they were believers, they were held slaves to sin because they were ignorant of the truth. This proves that Christians can be in bondage to darkness. If a demon can affect our minds, it can do an awful lot of damage. Look at what mental illness can do to people through affecting the mind. It can cause the person to have unspeakable desires and thoughts, and do unthinkable things!

God's love for us is very obvious for He sent His own Son to save sinners. Anybody who knows the message of the Cross has some knowledge of God's love for us. However, many times, we blame God for our problems, and so we forget the love He has for us. Not only do we blame Him for our tribulations, but many times we think that God gave us the trials to teach us a lesson. Nothing could be further from the truth! Jesus tells us clearly who came to hurt us and who came so that we could have life in abundance.

John 10:10;
10 The thief cometh not, but for to steal, and to kill, and to destroy: I am come that they might have life, and that they might have it abundantly.

Even the devil can disguise himself when approaching the children of God. Our defense is God, love and humility. Let us embrace the good news that no evil scheme can ruin us if we abide in the light of the glorious Gospel of true freedom, which is in Jesus Christ and Him alone.

2 Corinthians 4:6-12;
6 For God, who commanded the light to shine out of darkness, hath shined in our hearts, to give the light of the knowledge of the glory of God in the face of the Jesus Christ.

7 But we have this treasure in earthen vessels, that the excellency of the power may be of God, and not of us.

8 We are troubled on every side, yet not distressed; we are perplexed, but not in despair;

9 Persecuted, but not forsaken; cast down, but not destroyed;

10 Always bearing about in the body the dying of the Lord Jesus, that the life also of Jesus might be made manifest in our body.

11 For we which live are always delivered unto death for Jesus' sake, that the life also of Jesus might be manifest in our mortal flesh.

12 So then death worketh in us, but life is in you.

This is the only way out brethren. Allow no man to deceive you by calling you accursed for not paying this or that. Such is not a worker of love, but a liar with impure intentions. The Bible says in Acts 17:24-28;

24 God that made the world and all things therein, seeing that he is Lord of heaven and earth, dwelleth not in temples made by hands;

25 Neither is worshipped with men's hands, as though he needed anything, seeing he giveth to all life, and breath and all things;

26 And hath made of one blood all nations of men for to dwell on all the face of the earth, and hath determined the times before appointed, and the bounds of their habitation;

27 That they should seek the Lord if haply they might feel after him, and find him, though he be not far from every one of us:

28 For in him we live, and move, and have our being; as certain also of your own poets have said, For we are also his offspring.

2 Timothy 3:15;

15 And that from a child thou hast known the scriptures, which are able to make you wise unto salvation, which is of faith in Christ Jesus.

Brethren, now that you know the truth, I would like you to know that the way to get hold of it is by 'grace.' I would like you to keenly read this portion of the Bible.

Romans 5:1-21;

1 Therefore being justified by faith, we have peace with God through our Lord Jesus Christ:

2 By whom also we have access by faith into this grace wherein we stand and rejoice in hope of the glory of God.

3 And not only so, but we glory in tribulations also: knowing that tribulation worketh patience;

4 And patience, experience; and experience, hope:

5 And hope maketh not ashamed; because the love of God is shed abroad in our hearts by the Holy Ghost which is given unto us.

6 For when we were yet without strength, in due times Christ died for the ungodly.

7 For scarcely for a righteous will one die: yet peradventure for a good man some would even dare to die.

8 But God commendeth his love toward us, in that, while we were yet sinners, Christ died for us.

9 Much more then, being now justified by his blood we shall be saved wrath through Him.

10 For if, when we were enemies we were reconciled, we shall be saved by his life.

11 And not only so, but we also joy in God through our Lord Jesus Christ, by whom we have now received the atonement.

12 Wherefore, as by one man sin into the world, and death by sin; and so death passed upon all men, for that all have sinned:

13 For until the law sin was in the world: but sin is not imputed when there is no law.

14 Nevertheless death reigned from Adam to Moses, even over them that had not sinned after the similitude of Adam's transgression, who is the figure of him was to come.

15 But not as the offence, so also is the free gift. For if through the offence of one many are dead, much more the grace of God and the gift by grace which is by one man Jesus Christ hath abounded unto many.

16 And not as it was by one that sinned, so is the gift: for the judgment was by one to condemnation, but the free gift is of many offences unto justification.

17 For if by one man's offence death reigned by one; much more they which receive abundance of grace and of the gift of righteousness shall reign in life by one, Jesus Christ.

18 Therefore as by the offence of one judgment came upon all men to condemnation; even so by the righteousness of one the free gift came upon all men unto the justification of life.

19 For as by one man's disobedience many were be made righteous.

20 Moreover the law entered, that the offence might abound. But where sin abounded, grace did much more abound:

21 That as sin hath reigned unto death, even so might grace reign through righteousness unto eternal life by JESUS CHRIST our Lord.

Jesus foretold the welcome of the appearance of antichrist as follows: "*I am come in My Father's name, and ye receive me not: if another shall come in his own name, him ye will receive*", (John 5:43). It is impossible to reject the truth and escape enslavement to deception. Those who fall for false teachings have become inclined to 'the lie' by rejecting the truth. Christians today, in their quest for miracles and financial breakthroughs, have shut the windows of their hearts to the truth. Consequently, they have become poor, vulnerable victims of deceit. We all know that what God exposes, He is also able to redeem. Today, God wants to redeem the body from Abimelech-like men, but the question is, are you ready for this? If you are, then all you need to do is turn your backs from what you cherish the most, for it is nothing compared to the love of God. Even you, who are defending the lie because of material gain, need to discontinue. Stop being penny wise and pound foolish. There is no way your pastor can bless you more than Master JESUS. You have to say no and stand by your word otherwise you will be doomed too.

Notes and Reflections for Readers

THE BONE OF CONTENTION

There is a critical issue of disagreement that goes on within the Body of Christ. One group of people believe that salvation is by grace alone, a free gift which is by faith in Christ Jesus; as mentioned in Romans 3. The other group believes that salvation is not by faith alone, but by faith and works as it is written in James 2. This issue can mislead numerous people. Men who seek financial prosperity will ask remote questions instead of relevant questions relating to Jesus and the Church. Such people will tell you that salvation requires good deeds which include donating money, abstaining from certain foods, partaking of the physical sacrament of the holy eucharist, observing holy days, obeying the Ten Commandments, obeying superiors, and so on. Look brethren, no normal Christian filled with the Holy Spirit will contradict Paul, seeing the wisdom that was given to him by grace. Although Paul and James were talking about the same subject, faith and salvation, Paul holds that faith is the only imperative requirement for salvation while James says that faith, though a requirement unto salvation, must also bring forth good fruits. Both Paul and James turned to the life of Abraham to illustrate their justifications. Paul writes, "For if Abraham were justified by works, he hath whereof to glory; but not before God. For what saith the scripture? Abraham believed God, and it was counted unto him for righteousness." (Romans 4:2-3). James seems to contradict Paul when he writes, "Was not Abraham our father justified by works, when he had offered Isaac his son upon the altar?" (James 2:21).

A careful analysis will help shed light on this apparent disagreement. Paul makes it clear that it was faith alone that justified Abraham. He was referring to Genesis 15, where Abraham put his trust in the divine promise that he would be the father of many nations. God guaranteed the completion of His promise, thus Abraham was not justified by works of the law, but by faith when he believed God.

The event James is alluding to occurred in Genesis 22, when Abraham obediently offered Isaac as a sacrifice to fulfil God's command, until the last moment when God forbade him. It is notable that James also recites Genesis 15:6, thus inferring that Abraham was justified by faith earlier in his life, in agreement with Paul's teaching. James 2:24 states, "Ye see then how that by works a man is justified, and not by faith only." James teaches that Abraham was justified by works when he offered his son Isaac on the altar. Therefore, James is suggesting that Abraham was first justified by faith years before he was justified by works. Yet, the question remains, if Abraham was completely justified by faith, why must he be justified by deeds? The answer to this can be found by identifying the difference between what James and Paul meant by 'justification.' The emphasis in James is that faith is not living unless it is outwardly shown. "Yea, a man may say, Thou hast faith, and I have works: shew me thy faith without thy works, and I will shew thee my faith by my works." (James 2:18). This is because, as Paul states, faith is a personal belief that takes place in the mind and heart, and thus cannot be seen. Therefore, while God knows whether or not one has faith, there is no way for another person to recognize it exists unless there are works in his life that directly point to it. While Paul is dealing with the necessity of faith before God unto salvation, James is concerned with an outward demonstration of such faith before men through works. Therefore, unlike Paul, who teaches justification before God, James portrays justification before men. However, their views on justification are complementary. Paul stresses acceptance before God entirely by grace through faith, whereas James presents the continual evidence before men of the initial transaction.

Abraham's life was chosen as an example because it wonderfully illustrates what kind of faithful works James had in mind. Works in

James are the outworking of faith; if it's not a living faith, it becomes dead works. Abraham's work of faith was not only seen in his obedience to God's command, but also in the fact that he believed that God would raise up his son (Hebrews 11:19). God had promised Abraham that Isaac would have children and he believed that God would keep this promise even though God had commanded him to kill Isaac (Genesis 21:12). How can a dead Isaac have children? Abraham knew that the only solution to this impossible dilemma was that God would have to raise his son from the dead. Abraham's momentous faith in God's ability to fulfill His Word despite such difficulty is commended by the writer of Hebrews 11:19. Abraham's faith manifested itself in his willingness to obey God when all reason would repudiate his actions. This faith is seen as fruit of works of his previous faith which is unto salvation. Salvation by grace alone through faith is a broad and crucial topic; my next book will focus on this topic.

Notes and Reflections for Readers

NOTES AND REFLECTIONS FOR READERS

DESPISE NOT THE HOLY SPIRIT

The Holy Spirit of God is the third person of the God head, which is comprised of God the Father (the great I AM), God the Son which is Jesus Christ and God the Holy Spirit. The Holy Spirit is not a thing as some people suppose but a person, a spiritual person so to say, because He has not a physical human body. It possesses other human attributes as seen in the Bible, same like God the Father and God the Son. The Holy Spirit is not simply a force as the Jehovah's Witnesses and other cults profess, but a person. Although it has no physical human form, it has other human attributes as recorded in the Bible. The Bible tells us in Acts 13:2 that the Holy Spirit speaks.

2 As they ministered to the Lord, and fasted, the Holy Ghost said separate me Barnabas and Saul for the work whereunto I have called them.

We are told in Ephesians 4:30 that the Holy Spirit can be grieved.

30 And grieve not the Holy Spirit of God, whereby ye are sealed unto the day of redemption.

We also know that the Holy Spirit has a will in 1 Corinthians 12:11

11 But all these worketh that one and the selfsame spirit dividing to every man severally as he will.

When God the Father speaks forth the Word, which is Christ, it is the Holy Spirit that goes out to execute it. For example, in the Book of Genesis, we are told that when God was creating the world, He sent forth the Holy Spirit to create and renew the face of the earth (Psalms 104:30). It is the Spirit of God that created man as seen in the Book of Job 33:4.

After Jesus had eaten with His disciples during Passover, He told them that His mission was almost complete for He was about to be betrayed by one of them. Jesus told them that when He is gone, the Father will send them the Holy Spirit who will teach and remind them of all the things that were taught to them. He also said that the peace He gives them is not of this world. The Holy Spirit is the best teacher, one that you can trust for comfort and sound teachings. This is the spring of living water, the well that never dries up, that has been placed in the Spirit of every born again child of God. He is eager at all times to give you the Christ food and strengthen you. He is the shining light that shows you the golden path during those dark nights, and we all know how lonely life can get without His comfort. He is there to guide your spiritual walk and reawaken you to your true identity which is one with the Father through Christ. He speaks in numerous forms; in dreams, visions through the word of God, through the small voice from within etc.

The Holy Spirit is freely willing to live within those who believe in Jesus. In order to produce God's character in the life of a believer, which we cannot do on our own, the Holy Spirit will build into our lives love, peace, patience, faithfulness and self-control (Galatians 5:22-23). God asks us to walk in the Spirit and rely on Him to produce these qualities in our lives. The Holy Spirit empowers Christians to perform ministerial duties that promote spiritual growth among Christians and non-Christians. The Holy Spirit tugs on our hearts and minds, asking us to repent, and turn to God for forgiveness and a new life. In fact, when we preach to an unbeliever, it is the Holy Spirit alone who inspires them and turns their sinful heart unto Christ for repentance. The Holy Spirit also helps clean up our flaws. We do not always know what to pray for, so the Spirit Himself intercedes for us with cries that words cannot express (Romans 8:26).

You should not be puzzled, brethren, if a supposed Christian or a religious organization tells you they do not believe in the Holy Spirit and its power. Such is a cult and not from God. Those who are led by the Holy Spirit are children of God. The Bible says in John 14:16-17

"And I will pray the Father, and He will give you another Helper, that He may abide with you forever – The Spirit of truth, whom the world cannot receive, because it neither sees Him nor knows Him; but you know Him, for He dwells with you and will be in you."

NOTES AND REFLECTIONS FOR READERS

WHERE DO WE STAND WHEN EVERYTHING FAILS?

I t is a pity, such a breath snatching pity, seeing how the world is being ravaged by a few evil men who by their greed are chasing, money, power and the desire to enslave the entire human race; Africa being the chief sufferer. I am not a politician nor do I have to watch the BBC and CNN News daily to discover the dodgy arena we live in. Some years ago, I happened to be browsing the Internet when I came across an article that made my heart bleed. It was a story about Sarah "Saartjie" Baartman, a black woman from South Africa who had a very large buttocks. She was promised riches if she came to Europe, but instead was exhibited as a freak show attraction. Like an animal in a cage, she was forced to dance naked in London and Paris to please her audience. Her master would whip her if she resisted. The audience would touch, pinch and slap her buttocks. Her condition could only be compared to a caged animal in the zoo. Once the Parisians got tired of the Baartman show, she was forced to turn to prostitution and drinking in the streets of Paris, dying at the tender age 25 of an "inflammatory and eruptive sickness."

After she died, her body was cut up and studied by Napoleon's Doctor, Georges Cuvier. He made a cast of her body and put her skeleton, brain and labia in the Museum of Man in Paris where it was seen for more than one hundred years, until the 1970s. Some 160 years later, they were still on display, but were finally removed from public view in 1974. In 1994, President, Nelson Mandela, requested that her remains be brought home. Other representations were made, but it took the French government eight years to pass a bill, apparently worded so not to prevent other countries from claiming the return of their stolen treasures, to allow their small piece of "scientific curiosity" to be returned to South Africa. In January 2002, Sarah Baartman's remains were returned and buried on 9 August 2002, on South Africa's Women's Day, at Hankey in the Eastern Cape Province. Her grave has since been declared a national heritage site.

Today, Africa is plagued with the deadly man made ebola, and even more is the fact that sadly America chooses to send 3000 foot soldiers to combat the disease rather than send medical doctors. A lot of evil is happening in the world today, that would shock even the devil. The West is becoming more like Sodom and Gomorrah. I even read a whacky article where an Indian girl married a dog to remove bad luck and ensure benevolence of the village. What a bizarre tribal ritual! When Obama came into power, blacks worldwide were ecstatic that finally someone of black origin could plead their cause as he would feel the plight of blacks in America, he himself being black. Sadly, their dreams and expectations were thrown into the dark cave of broken hearts when they soon found out that Obama was simply a man serving a higher authority.

So much evil goes on in the world today. Powerful people will silently push groups of people from another nation to mobilize against their brothers. How, you ask? All they need to do is brandish them with a name, finance and equip them militarily. Then later on, they will appear in the scene as though they are come to make peace, whereas beyond the surface, they are cunningly robbing the country of its mineral resources. Money sold Jesus, so it is no surprise that foolish men on earth today will adopt evil behavior still for the sake of money. The bible says there is nothing new under the sun.

The weak shall be made strong. Yes, someday, but only by the strength of the Almighty God. You have probably heard it being said that man's search for freedom is unending, but I tell you, that is the lie of the devil. Is there a means to an end of man's predicament and bondage?

Oh yes there is, and the only way out is by the Lord God Almighty; no more, no less. For how can darkness be exposed by another form of darkness? Impossible! Darkness can only make another dark situation worse. This is the reason why Libyans have got their hands on their head right now. When light reveals itself, darkness is swallowed up in light and the filth of darkness is brought to the sight of people. Darkness, not being able to conquer light, will automatically bow in shame. That is true freedom. It is achieved not by power, but by the Spirit of the most high Man; it is a 90% spiritual battle and only 10% physical, so it must be approached spiritually relating to the Lord and His host, not of fist and iron.

Again, I am not a politician and politics does not interest me in any way, but my business is love and freedom of the lost, weak and oppressed. Sometimes, I really wonder what men have exchanged their God given hearts for. All this fame, money and greatness are temporal and short-term. If your definition of greatness has to do with enslavement and betraying others, then that's a cruel reflection of you. True greatness is not gathered from one's intellect or ability to charm people with fine deceitful words. A true fruit of the Spirit springs from the gift of love. It is best expressed in one's willingness to give all and die defending a just cause in a Godly way. Men like Jesus Christ, Moses, Martin Luther, Marcus Garvey, Frederick Douglass and John Wesley portray God's pure motives.

We can see how the devil is using our own black brothers and sisters to spread luciferianism within the music industry. Much more unspeakable evil is taking place in the world today, but we supposed men of God keep quiet. Oh, how my heart bleeds for our lost brothers and sisters, like Lil Wayne, Jay-Z and Rihanna, all chasing fame and forgetting their Soul. How I wish God would give true servants the grace and accompany me into the ghettos and slums of America where black brothers are lost and dead to the addiction of drugs and other horrible sins, in frustration, that they might find peace and truth, in Him, Christ, that they could hear the truth that speaks of them in Christ and be made whole and alive again. I pray this becomes reality someday. It is a great pity that we are not affected enough by the way the world has turned out. We do not cry out or fall on our knees and intercede for the world, because we are not our own pure selves anymore. We have sold ourselves to the lust of money and become its servant.

In the midst of all these things, what do we do? What is our solution? Who do we turn to for help when no one seems to be listening and no one is wise enough to acknowledge the difference between right and wrong? Is it America, is it the WHO or is it the European Union? Neither, for they are all of the same accord attempting to achieve the same worthless purposes. You do not need people to change your story or turn things around for you; all you who are broken-hearted and downtrodden, Africa most especially, need one man, just one, His name is JESUS. Seek Him personally in prayers and supplications, in private studies and research. Cry out for His visitation. I did that, and only when we do that with humility, all children of mother Africa will find true freedom that is so close now, though it seems far. The Bible says in Jeremiah 17:5

5 Thus saith the Lord; Cursed be the man that trusteth in man, and maketh flesh his arm, and whose heart departeth from the Lord.

God is our only hope. The battle is more of the Spirit. At the mention of the name of the Lord Jesus, every knee and every situation must bow. John 14:13-14 confirms this.

13 And whatsoever ye shall ask in my name, that will I do, that the father may be glorified in the son.
14 If ye shall ask anything in my name, I will do it.

The God of yesterday who took the Israelites out from bondage in Egypt with the staff of a shepherd is still the same God today. We can do even more wonderful things if we trust and hold onto Him. He is seeking men to use in this hour to turn situations around. Are you ready? If yes, then make yourself available. Stand in patience, faith and honesty; even in persecutions, remain strong and faithful.

Notes and Reflections for Readers

THE PAINFUL IRONY OF BISHOP DAVID'S SHILOH 2014 AND THE OLD FASHIONED BLOOD

Upon completing *The Great Outcry*, I received an invite to the Shiloh International all night program conducted by Mr. David Oyedepo. The program is usually held once a year in Nigeria at the Winners Chapel headquarters. What I witnessed there moved me to write an additional two chapters. The theme of this Shiloh program was 'Heaven on Earth.' Living in Belgium meant I had to go to the Winners Chapel of Brussels. It took about one hour and thirty minutes to get there from Leuven; I travelled by bus, metro then by bus again. I arrived at about 9:00pm, a bit early, so we had to wait for the other church members who were still on their way coming. They arrived and we started singing praise and worship songs followed by prayers. Over three hours later, we were connected to the main branch in Nigeria, a very big Chapel which held thousands of people that night. We continued from there, joining the main branch in worship for about an hour, after which Mr. Oyedepo took the floor to deliver the message to his people. His sermon went for about two hours, but what pulled my attention the most was the sprinkling of blood on the people. Elders were instructed to come forward with bowls carrying water turned red by syrup and were instructed to sprinkle the water (blood) on everyone present at the service. Bishop David Oyedepo read out Hebrews 9:19

19 For when Moses had spoken every precept to all the people according to the law, he took the blood of calves and of goats, with water, and scarlet wool and hyssop, and sprinkled both the book, and all the people.

After he had finished reading the verse, he made declarations in a prophetic way. He said, "I decree by partaking of the sprinkling that every broken marriage will be made whole, every sickness will be healed, and financial doors will open, and so on."

When the elders started sprinkling the blood, I left the Church hall and came back once they had finished the exercise because to me it was a very useless act and definitely didn't see myself partaking of it. After the Church service, I went up to the pastor and in the course of our discussion I told him that I did not partake of the blood sprinkling practice, because I am new to the Winners Chapel and do not understand the practice. He told me that it is Biblical and that I should not be afraid as the water in the bowls were made red by ordinary syrup to appear like blood. He quoted Exodus 12:13-14 and told me that it is an old practice by the Israelites in the days of Moses for the remission of sins.

13 And the blood shall be to you for a token upon the houses where ye are: and when I see the blood, I will pass over you, and the plague shall not be upon you to destroy you, when I smite the land of Egypt.

14 And this day shall be unto you for a memorial; and ye shall keep it a feast to the Lord throughout your generations; ye shall keep it a feast by an ordinance for ever.

I told him but this was done in the Old as he rightly said. We have a better assurance now in the New, the Blood of the Lamb of God, which is Jesus Christ, which was instituted to replace the old blood of animals.

1 Peter 1:18-23;

18 Forasmuch as ye know that ye were not redeemed with corruptible things, as silver and gold, from your vain conversation received by tradition from your fathers;

19 But with the precious blood of Christ, as of a lamb without blemish and without spot:

20 Who verily was foreordained before the foundation of the world, but was manifest in these last times for you,

21 Who by him do believe in God, that raised him up from the dead, and gave him glory; that your faith and hope might be in God.

22 Seeing ye have purified your souls in obeying the truth through the spirit unto unfeigned love of the brethren, see that ye love one another with a pure heart fervently:

23 Being born again, not of the corruptible seed, but of incorruptible by the word of God, which liveth and abideth for ever.

Verse 18 says that we were not redeemed with corruptible things. Brethren, we need to start thinking and acting straight. Your money did not and will never save you from the power of the devil. Neither will the traditions of Old you received from your forefathers, which entail sacrificing animals for the atonement of sins. These were all shadow things of the Old that all pointed to the New which is Christ the Messiah. He alone is the sole requirement; He is that true ram that was promised in Genesis 22. Remember when Abraham took his long awaited son, Isaac, the love of his heart, to sacrifice in the land of Moriah. On their way to the mountain, Isaac asked his father a very important question. He noted that they had the knife, the wood and the fire, but they did not have the animal for the sacrifice. Abraham's reply was that God will provide. When they got to the place of sacrifice, Abraham set up the wood for the sacrifice then tied his son to the altar; ready to kill him when God intervened and stopped him. God told Abraham to turn around, and there behind him was a big ram that was caught by the horns in a thicket. God was telling us here that a lamb will come from Abraham, the Isaac to be slaughtered, but for the time being Isaac had to live in order for the lamb, Christ to be sacrificed at the appointed time. Brethren, we really have to study the Word with knowledge from the Spirit. This important revelation will set us free.

I desired to talk more with the pastor, but he gave me little chance to say a word, stopping me every now and again. I was shocked when he finally said the red syrup that was sprinkled was the Blood of Christ. Brethren, it is time for us to choose whether to stand for men and justify their actions or to stand for God. If we know the truth, let us proclaim it; none of these lies in exchange for material gain and popularity. God is faithful and able to reward us spiritually and materially. Those who defend His name and cause justly will receive every necessity at the right time, but even if He does not grant what we desire, no problem at all, that means we were not destined to have great material substance. He knows best. We should overcome our canal man and lust for materialism, and bring it under subjection to the will of God. Only then can we say that we are God's devoted servants. A faithful servant is one who is loyal to no one else but his Master alone. He cannot be enticed or brought under the control of material things that will make him lose his faithfulness. Money is good and a necessity indeed, but how tasteful it is to give ourselves wholly for LOVE. Yes of course, the love for God and for the lost so that we can live the Christly life, the same life that Christ lived and tasted in the bodily form. How gloriously sweet it is; there can be nothing more fulfilling and peaceful from the inside out. If you read the Book of Hebrews 9:10-24, you will get a clearer understanding of the point I am trying to make as opposed to the verse read by Mr. Oyedepo (Hebrews 9:19).

Hebrews 9:10-24

10 Which stood only in meats and drinks, and divers washings, and carnal ordinances, imposed on them until the time of reformation.

11 But Christ being come an high priest of good things to come, by a greater and more perfect tabernacle, not made with hands, that is to say, not of this building;

12 Neither by the blood of goats and calves, but by his own blood he entered in once into the holy place, having obtained eternal redemption for us.

13 For if the blood of bulls and of goats, and the ashes of an heifer sprinkling the unclean, sanctifieth to the purifying of the flesh:

14 How much more shall the blood of Christ, who through the eternal spirit offered himself without spot to God, purge your conscience from dead works to serve the living God?

15 And for this cause he is the meditator of the new testament, that by means of death, for the redemption of the transgression that were under the first testament, they which are called might receive the promise of the eternal inheritance.

16 For where a testament is, there must also be of necessity the death of the testator.

17 For a testament is of force after men are dead: otherwise it is of no strength at all while the testator liveth.

18 Whereupon neither the first testament was dedicated without blood.

19 For when Moses had spoken every precept to all people according to the law, he took the blood of calves and of goats with water and scarlet wool and hyssop, and sprinkled both the book, and all the people.

20 Saying, This is the blood of the testament which God hath enjoined unto you.

21 Moreover he sprinkled with blood both the tabernacle, and all the vessels of the ministry.

22 And almost all things are by the law purged with blood; and without shedding of blood is no remission.

23 It was therefore necessary that the patterns of things in the heavens should be purified with these; but the heavenly things themselves with better sacrifices than these.

24 For Christ is not entered into the holy places made with hands, which are the figures of the true; but into heaven itself now to appear in the presence of God for us:

Although the sprinkling of blood is biblical, as was practiced yearly by men of the Old for the atonement of sins, it has been replaced by the Blood of Christ whom the prophets of the Old prophesied, alluding to Jesus Christ of the New Covenant, the true Lamb of God. We have now been ushered into the Holy of Holies; all of us by faith are born again in Jesus Christ. The original shadow of the Holy of Holies was only accessible by the high priests on behalf of the people. Therefore, we become penny wise and pound foolish, to turn back to the ways of the Old, and be loyal again once more to the high priests of old when we have been privileged and highly favored to be set free from their monopoly of power and assess to the holies of holies through the law, by way of true freedom in Christ Jesus. Why be misled by a handful of supposed guardians who hide behind greed? After all this, I decided to do some research on Mr. Oyedepo and his Shiloh scheme. I found an interesting piece of material on the Internet, a preamble of the Shiloh program of 2012 by Bishop David Oyedepo.

PREAMBLE

We are in the last days and the era of double portion in the Body of Christ. We are the Elisha generation of the New Testament Church. We are called to earnestly covet the grace that was placed upon the men and women who have gone before us. The "Spirits of just men made perfect" is being unleashed upon the end time Saints in full force. The same way Elisha cried out saying, "... I pray thee, let a double portion of thy spirit be upon me," and God heard him with testimony. This should be the experience of every one at Shiloh 2012. Every one shall return home with a double portion of the Spirit upon God's servant and upon this commission.

Remember, this is the 14th Shiloh and we look forward to a wave of supernatural manifestations, the kind we have never seen before. Also note, "The husbandman that laboureth shall be the first partaker of the fruit." (2 Tim 2:6) Therefore, the more fervent we are in prayers, the greater the portion of individuals shall be at Shiloh 2012."

Brethren, permit me to reveal the truth. This is all junk and a carefully mapped out scheme to brainwash and manipulate the people who have refused to seek the truth for themselves. They have refused to draw out true and living water from the ceaseless spring which exists within. Remember 1 John 2:27 says, "But the anointing which ye have received of him abideth in you, and ye need not that any man teach you: but as the same anointing teacheth you of all things, and is truth, and is no lie, and even as it hath taught you, ye shall abide in him."

Whether you accept it or not, Mr. Oyedepo is trying to present himself as an icon, a great oracle so to say, capable of giving the people a double portion of anointing; the way Elisha received from Elijah the moment he was transported to Heaven. This is practically impossible as this was done by God alone in the Old. The order of things has changed, and the Old ways have been replaced with the New. Every man called by God has been granted a unique anointing which is relevant to his area of calling. It is a free gift from God and does not depend on how much the man prayed as our five fingers are not the same, or as our faces or finger prints are not the same so does our anointing differ from one another. Mark this, any person who promises to give you a double portion of his anointing will only leave you disappointed and with less money in your pocket.

Anointing is from God by the Spirit not from man. There are two possible reasons behind these misguided teachings. Either he is ignorant of what the Word of God says regarding anointing in this New Testament era of grace or he is a thief. The Bible says in 1 John 2:20, "But ye have an unction from the Holy One, and ye know all things."

NOTES AND REFLECTIONS FOR READERS

NOTES AND REFLECTIONS FOR READERS

A RELEVANT MESSAGE RELATING TO SHILOH IN THIS ERA

Shiloh was the religious capital of Israel during the times of the Judges, and spans 4,000 years of continuous settlement starting from the 18th C BC (Middle Bronze II). Shiloh was an assembly place for the people of Israel and a center of worship. That is where the tabernacle stood before the temple was built in Jerusalem. The Ark of the Covenant was there, and somehow, the people were convinced that if the Ark was physically present with them, then they were invincible. They were not faithful to the Lord in their conduct and service, but depended on their 'magical Ark,' to prevail in battle against the Philistines.

They were wrong about that. It was at Shiloh where the Ark of the Covenant was captured by the Philistines and the unfaithful people of Israel were defeated (1 Samuel 4:10-11). It was as if they believed that the Ark was a lamp and God was a genie inside, enslaved to whoever possessed the Ark. That was a mistake.

For those who know the history of Shiloh in the Book of 1 Samuel, Shiloh brings to the Israelites a sad memory. In His anger and grief, God decided to release the Israelites into the hands of the Philistines in a bloody battle in which the Israelites camped at Ebenezer and the Philistines at Aphek. We are told in the Book of 1 Samuel 2:12-35 that the sons of Eli were scoundrels with no regard for the Lord and the priests' customs. This was a grave sin before the Lord for they abhorred the offering of the Lord.

A man of God was sent to Eli, to warn him of his sons' evil deeds, that they may turn away and repent. If not, the days will come when God will cut off Eli's strength and the strength of his father's house, so that no man will grow old in that house. The man who survives such suffering will be left with tears of sorrow and loneliness to deal with the loss of his descendants. As a sign, both sons, Hophni and Phinehas shall die on the same day. God will raise an anointed, faithful priest who will do His will, and God will build him a steady house forever.

This warning from God was directed at the priests, but they did not yield, so just as the servant of God had spoken, the Philistines went into battle against the Israelites and Israel's army was smitten before the Philistines. In the field, they slew about four thousand men. Inside the camp, the elders of Israel discussed the need to fetch the Ark of the Covenant out of Shiloh, the only thing that might save them from the hands of their enemies. When the Ark of the Covenant of the Lord came into the camp, all of Israel shouted with a great shout, so that the earth rang again.

The Philistines fought and Israel was smitten, and they fled every man into his tent. It was an immense slaughter leaving thirty thousand foot soldiers dead. The Ark of God was taken and Eli's two sons, Hophni and Phinehas, were slain. The City cried out in anguish. When Eli heard the noise of the crying, his dim eyes and frail stability at the age of ninety-eight, wept for answers. He was informed that Israel fled from the Philistines after a great slaughter took place among the people, his two sons were killed and the Ark of God was taken. When Eli heard the Ark of God was robbed, his heavy weight lost balance and he fell backwards breaking his neck. He died an old man. His daughter-in-law, Phinehas' wife, was with child, near to be delivered. When she heard the news that the Ark of God was taken, and that her father-in-law and husband were dead, she bowed herself and went into labor, for her pains came upon her. The Philistines took the Ark of God and brought it from Ebenezer into the house of Ashdod, their god.

How I wish today's organizers of the annual Shiloh program were to cry out heavily, seeking the servants of God who have gone astray to come back into the original position of good fate, honesty and sincerity.

The past tragedy that befell the people of Israel, as a result of the evil deeds of the sons of Eli, should remain a life lesson. How I wish they would stand in the place of Samuel and cry out to the world to bring back their fidelity to God. Israel was plunged into wanton catastrophe at the feet of the Philistines, just because the priests, sons of Eli were pressing to take by force from the people what did not belong to them, robbing them, and using the sacrifices offered to God as instructed by God, they were corrupt and perverse in their ways. Today, like never before, we hear of greedy preachers turning the Scripture completely upside down, knowingly in a bid to extort money from the people of God. One such soulless man, by the name of Morris Cerullo, even dared to come up with his own Bible entitled 'Financial Freedom Bible', and the children of God are rushing for it, what a joke ! what do you guys think you are doing ? Look people, no such thing should be considered. Only the true revelation knowledge of the Word of God, given by the Spirit of God, can bring forth true freedom in every area of our lives. Do not listen to what these men are telling you, they are a bunch of criminals. I am not claiming to be the most holy or righteous man, far from it, I too am a sinner with my own weaknesses. I just thank God for His grace and assurance of true freedom and liberation by the cross of Jesus Christ. Like Apostle Paul said, "And lest I should be exalted above measure through the abundance of the revelations, there was given to me a thorn in the flesh, the messenger of Satan to buffet me, lest I should be exalted above measure." (2 Corinthians 12:7).

Today, God is speaking to all of you. Preachers of today who have set aside the key things pertaining to the kingdom of God, for temporary things, God is saying that if you repent and turn from your old ways, it will be well with you. Reject the vain and worthless path you are on and come back home. Your nakedness will be covered once more with the glorious garments of pure love, faith, hope, truth and charity. How can you have peace of mind sleeping on a poorly made bed of dollar bills? How can you ignore the cries of the poor you robbed of their hard earnings when they trusted you? How can you hold back the grace and glory of God from shining upon the people, and not feel remorse? Our job is to shame darkness and enlighten people to the truth. Any legacy built upon guile is nothing but shame. Turn away from it, deny it and embrace a true path that comes with inner peace, joy and freedom. What I speak of comes from the mind of the Lord God Almighty. You have the choice to believe or not to believe, to yield or not to yield. The finger of God is pointing in a very loud voice to all you manipulators, and partners of deceit in America, Europe, Africa and the world at large. Enough is enough; you are countless and must repent. A lot has been echoed to you before now, but you seem to return deaf ears. Let he who is wise and prudent listen to the warnings of *The Great Outcry*. REPENT is a word sufficient to the wise. Let us read the words of Revelations 3:1-6;

1 And unto the angel of the church in Sardis write; these things saith he that hath the seven spirits of God, and the seven stars; I know thy works, that thou hast a name that thou livest and art dead.

2 Be watchful, and strengthen the things which remain, that are ready to die: for I have not found thy works perfect before God.

3 Remember therefore how thou hast received and heard, and hold fast and repent. If therefore thou shalt not know what hour I will come upon thee.

4 Thou hast a few names even in Sardis which have not defiled their garments; and they shall walk with me in white:

for they are worthy.

5 He that overcometh, the same shall be clothed in white raiment; and I will not blot out his name out of the book of life, but I will confess his name before my father, and before his angels.

6 He that hath an ear, let him hear what the spirit saith, unto the churches.

You may say but who am I and who gives me the audacity to speak my mind to 'great men of God.' Sometimes, I even wonder how and why, considering I am no better than the next person. To a certain extent, we are all right, but to a far greater extent, we are all wrong. Someone may seem to be nobody in the eyes of someone else, but he is definitely somebody to the all-knowing and Almighty Heavenly

Creator. I may indeed be nobody to you and even to me, but to Christ, I am somebody through His power and His grace, that is the same spirit I desire every child of God to have see yourselves as Christ and no liar will deceive and manipulate you, for indeed you are one with Him.

! Corinthians 6:17 says: But he that is joined unto the Lord is one spirit and ! Corinthians 12 :27 says; Now ye are the body of Christ, and members in particular.

Some years ago why I was still in Libya after my usual evening prayers I slept and in the course of sleeping, I had a dream in which in the course of the dream, I saw an angel of the Lord appeared unto me and said to me who was lying down on the floor in a church let sleeping and blind eyes be opened, immediately some scales fell from my eyes onto the ground. Now God was in this dream, not opening my fleshly and carnal eyes, but my spiritual eyes, that I may begin to see and comprehend the hidden mystery in the word of God. In like manner I pray that God will open the eyes of every true seeker of the truth in this glorious era in which we operate of which he said "Ash and it shall be given to you, seek and you will find; knock and the door will be opened to you" (Mathew 7:7).

Your money conscious men will tell you knock, seek and ask and God will open the doors of financial riches unto you but no, Christ was talking about opening the doors to the kingdom of God, this has to do with revealing the hidden truths to you. This was the keys to heaven Christ was talking about when he told Peter that he was giving him the keys of heaven, and not some giant physical keys. God is Spirit remember, and He is referring always to spiritual things even when He talking about physical things.

Notes and Reflections for Readers

Printed in the United States
By Bookmasters